WOMEN
WHO CHANGED
THE HEART
OF THE CITY

12308

WOMEN WHO CHANGED THE HEART OF THE CITY

The Untold Story of the City Rescue Mission Movement

DELORES T. BURGER

kregel
PUBLICATIONS

Grand Rapids, MI 49501

Women Who Changed the Heart of the City: The Untold Story of the City Rescue Mission Movement

Copyright © 1997 by Delores T. Burger

Published by Kregel Publications, a division of Kregel, Inc., P.O. Box 2607, Grand Rapids, MI 49501. Kregel Publications provides trusted, biblical publications for Christian growth and service. Your comments and suggestions are valued.

For more information about Kregel Publications, visit our web site at http://www.kregel.com.

Cover design: PAZ Design Group
Book design: Nicholas G. Richardson

Library of Congress Cataloging-in-Publication Data
Burger, Delores.
    Women who changed the heart of the city: the untold story of the city rescue mission movement / Delores Burger.
        p.   cm.
    Includes bibliographical references and index.
    1. Women missionaries—Biography. 2. City Missions—History. I. Title.
BV2657.A1B87   1997   267'.13'0922—dc20   96-32054
                                                        CIP

ISBN 0-8254-2146-2

Printed in the United States of America

2 3 4 / 03 02 01 00 99 98 97

To my mother,
who taught me how to
love God and my neighbor

Bessy Latuff Prohofsky

Everyone loves a story, and everyone finds encouragement from role models—heroes of the faith. And this is what Delores Burger provides us with in her book, *Women Who Changed the Heart of the City*.

As you read, you will encounter women, ordinary women, who were mightily used of God because they moved according to God's gifting and calling upon their lives in their unique role—designed as women by the Almighty. And in this encounter we pray you will catch a vision, a vision for the heart of your city and God's call upon your life.

—Kay Arthur

Contents

Preface

❧··❧

his is a significant book about women in history who have been integral to rescue ministries, starting with Frances Nasmith in the early 1800s, followed by other women probably not well known to us—Emma Whittemore, Sarah Clarke, and Clemme Ellis White, to name several. These women have been city missionaries with extraordinary effectiveness. This book helps us to know these women face-to-face. Of course, these women ministers did not seek attention for themselves. In fact, they might be embarrassed by a book that features them. But there are compelling reasons for describing them. For one thing, their stories have remained hidden from us, and a light is not to be kept "under a bushel." It is refreshing to become aware of these women and their heroic role in rescue ministries. Furthermore, they were remarkable women, and accounts of their work inspire all involved in Christian service. The earthly ministries of these "compassionate, committed, and courageous" women are ended, but reading here about their lives and observing the work of God in them serves to continue their ministry among us.

IVAN J. FAHS, PH.D.
Professor of Sociology
Wheaton College

Acknowledgments

❧·❧

This book came out of a passionate desire the Lord placed in my heart. First that desire was to tell how God changes lives. Second, to show how God has used changed lives to change the heart of cities around the world through the last two centuries.

During a dinner conversation with Dr. Ivan Fahs and my husband, I shared the woman's role in urban ministry. Ivan stated with enthusiasm, "You have to tell that story. It would make a good book."

In telling the story I have been constrained by space, for each of these saints deserves a whole book and to some I could only give two pages. I tried to use their words so you could feel their heartbeat; thus, some of the language is of a different era.

This book would not exist without the love, encouragement, writing, and editing of my dear husband, Steve. Our daughter, Linda, her husband, John Neudorf; our son, Eric, his wife, Robbyn; and our grandchildren, Erica Faith and Caren Hope, have given me joy and help in many ways.

So many encouraged and helped me that it is hard to make a list, but the following went that extra mile, and I appreciate it: Mary Bergeman, Dr. Ivan Fahs, Mrs. Charles Furness, Dennis Hillman, Myron Hilty, Frank Koop, Thomas Laymon, Dr. and Mrs. Malcolm Lee, Alison Ogran, Jessica Ogran, Bonnie Robertson, Mr. and Mrs. Robert Robertson, Anita Seaburg, Terry Whitley, Rachel Warren, and the staff of both the IUGM and Kregel Publications.

Introduction

➤·◄

In the inner city today, yet another child is killed in a drug-related shooting." The television reporter tells how many people will die of AIDS by the year 2000, and then he says, "Stay tuned for a special report on unmarried teenage moms and their babies. . . ." In a world that is filled with evil, fear, anger, and hate, how do Christians respond?

As we enter the twenty-first century, we can look back one hundred years to a time when Christians responded in a dynamic way to desperate social and spiritual conditions. That response was a revolution in American Christianity. "Proper" people left the pews of the church and went to the squalor of the city. Dwight L. Moody, the greatest evangelist of the nineteenth century, challenged people to care for the poor and the broken. Jerry McAuley opened the Water Street Mission in New York City with the help of the president of the New York Stock Exchange. The Good Samaritan call was alive, and people were responding not just in preaching and teaching but in going to the bowels of the city, loving the unlovely and bringing the Gospel in word and deed to the alcoholic, the prostitute, the broken, and the forgotten.

First a stream, then a river; hundreds of people from all walks of life became part of a great movement of God committed to changing the heart of the city. The movement became known as the rescue mission movement, and from a small beginning it has grown to a movement that today is in almost every city of size in America, with a companion city mission movement in many of the great cities of the world.

By 1913, just forty years after their beginning, there were over five hundred rescue missions in the United States and Canada. Tonight, over thirty thousand men, women, boys, and girls will sleep in rescue mission facilities, and over one hundred thousand meals will be served to the hungry in North America. Three hundred fifty million dollars will be raised and spent this year on the poor by rescue

15

missions that are members of the International Union of Gospel Missions (IUGM) in the United States and Canada. These missions represent a great movement of God with a humble, exciting, and most unusual beginning.

Throughout history rescue missions have been founded and operated by unlikely people. Jerry McAuley was a converted alcoholic ex-con with little education. Some founders were socialites and pastors, some were society's misfits, and, to the surprise of even many in the movement today, many were women. In 1946 fifty rescue missions in America had women as their directors and, according to Dr. W. E. Paul, author of *Romance of Rescue*, were "some of the very best" missions. When women were not directors, they were the field workers, the ones who went to the jails and who set up the soup kitchens. They also, as in the case of "Ma" Clarke, cofounder of Chicago's Pacific Garden Mission, were the inspiration behind the founding and "mother" to thousands, including, in Ma Clarke's case, famed evangelists Billy Sunday and Mel Trotter. In some cases these women were the unsung heroes, working with their husbands who got much of the credit and fame. But more than that, these women were the heart of this great movement.

The apostle Paul stated in 1 Thessalonians 2:6–7, "As apostles of Christ we could have been a burden to you, but we were gentle among you, like a mother caring for her little children." The mother's heart is a special heart. It believes the best, it hopes for the best, and it forgives when failure comes. A mother's love never quits or gives up. It follows the prodigal and the broken. It takes a woman where often men have feared to go. Mothers have special hearts filled with compassion, commitment, and courage.

The Bible tells us that "God is love" (1 John 4:16), and "Thou shalt love the Lord thy God with all thy heart, and with all thy soul, and with all thy mind. This is the first and greatest commandment. And the second is like unto it, "Thou shalt love thy neighbor as thyself. On these two commandments hang all the law and the prophets" (Matt. 22:37–40 KJV).

The women of rescue are an indispensable but often forgotten force in a great Christian spiritual and social movement not just in America but in the major cities of the developed world. Theirs is the untold story, and it needs to be told.

This great city rescue mission movement began in Scotland in 1826 and history records its founder as one David Nasmith, a sickly bookkeeper who founded the Glasgow City Mission, the London City Mission, and the Dublin City Mission, all still in operation today. Until now little has been written about Frances Nasmith, wife of

David. When David died at age forty, Frances was a young widow
with five children. And then there was Maria McAuley . . . but let's
not get ahead of our untold story.

STEVE BURGER
Executive Director, IUGM

1

Overcome Evil with Good

David Nasmith, Founder of City Missions

*Few matches have been more equal and seldom has more depended on
such equality. . . . She was truly a helpmate to her husband, with a
heart as large and a zeal as ardent as David had himself. . . . Her
Christian virtue and moral courage did not fail.*
—John Campbell

Introduction

Then Jesus entered a house, and again a crowd gathered, so that he and his disciples were not even able to eat. When his family heard of this, they went to take charge of him, for they said, "He is out of his mind" Mark 3:20–21.

*Y*ou must be crazy! You're out of your mind! You're going to do what? Give up your position and your security to go work with those people? They want to be like that—don't waste your life on them." Non-Christians and Christians often respond this way when someone follows the call of the Lord to work with the thief, the prostitute, the poor, and the needy.

What drives some people with the passion, determination, and certainty that reaching their goal is everything to them to the point of ridicule, failure, and humiliation? All logic and common sense seem to be gone. The great intellectual minds say it can't be done. They are mad, those dreamers! But then it seems like a miracle; they reach their goal! For years Thomas Edison gathered different substances from all over the world at great cost before he found the right one for the filament of the light bulb that changed the world. An unlikely young Scot shared the same sort of drive for a far different vision.

The information in this chapter is taken from John Campbell's *Memoirs of David Nasmith: His Labours and Travels in Great Britain, France, and the United States and Canada* (London: John Snow, 1844).

It was laughable when David Nasmith, an uneducated, sickly, young bookkeeper, went in his leisure time to the disease-infested slums, visiting thieves, prostitutes, the poor and needy, to bring moral change to the cities of the world. Some said he was crazy, but that was his vision, his goal! And Frances Hartridge must have been out of her mind when she married David, who gave money away to the point of poverty. What did Frances Hartridge see in David Nasmith? She suffered hardship, poor health, and humiliation as she shared her life with him. Some say they burned themselves out, but because of them the lights of the city missions around the world still shine brightly some 170 years later. Dr. John Campbell likened Nasmith's reformer role to that of Xavier, Knox, Calvin, Luther, and Wesley (pp. 432–36). All could be called godly men, sinners and saints, who found salvation to be the pivotal spark in their lives.

David Nasmith was born March 21, 1799 in Glasgow, Scotland. When he was eleven years old his teacher told his parents, "David has spent four years learning absolutely nothing. He doesn't like language and won't even try." So David became a bound apprentice to a pious manufacturer. Soon, however, the business was sold to a wicked man, and David was sold like machinery in the deal, a little boy caught up in the evils of the industrial revolution. These were years of great danger for the moral and religious principles that he had learned at his mother's knee, because the evil man's business abounded with wickedness.

David wrote,

> When I look back to the many sins which I then committed, unknown to man, they make me tremble! When tempted, I often prayed to God for deliverance; but sin remained as a sweet morsel under my tongue (p. 4).

Through his apprenticeship years David went to Sabbath school, and when two of his Sabbath school friends wanted to form a society for the distribution of Bibles, they asked David to be their secretary.

> I made friends with a number of pious young men, whose walk and conversation were very consistent, which led me to often think upon the contents of the Bibles we were giving to others. I found an increasing interest in what it said; I was led to see myself as a guilty polluted sinner, in the sight of an infinitely pure and holy God, and my heart desperately wicked, and unable to do any thing to satisfy Divine justice. Often did I try to improve my conduct; but as often did I find that, as the leopard cannot change its spots, no more can they who have been accustomed to do evil learn to do well. By continuing to search the Scriptures, I found One, even Jesus, who could deliver not only from the punishment, but from the power of sin. He appeared altogether as the one I stood in need of—a Savior all-sufficient—yes, mighty to save! (pp. 3–7).

Salvation is the spark of vision, the ability to see. In every century there is a struggle between good and evil, between God and the Devil! It is won or lost in the human heart. We cannot understand evil without understanding sin. Yet as David found out, there is a Savior, a God of love who can help us "overcome evil with good" (Rom. 12:21).

Out of David's honest testimony from the heart of a sinner saved by grace came the vision for two great movements: first, the YMCA,

which was intended for those up to the age of fourteen and was an
outgrowth of his Sabbath school, or Sunday school; the second was
the city mission movement.

David wrote to the "dear boys" who had been in his Sunday school
classes who had found employment in other cities:

> Dear William! What think you now of Jesus? I have been
> visiting occasionally three young men who this day are put
> to death in front of the jail. We might well say, "There go
> David Nasmith and William Somerville, save for the grace
> of God" (p. 81). It has been proposed to form an association
> among the young men, which is likely to take place. I hope
> to have the pleasure of the company of the whole to break-
> fast. . . . Dr. Wardlaw addresses the young people on the
> forenoon of New Year's day, at eleven o'clock, in the Lower
> Trades Hall (p. 83). Young men who were favorably disposed
> to religion, but not decided, have been won to Christ; those
> who in business, or otherwise, were necessarily associated
> with the infidel and licentious youth of their own age, or
> with masters of iniquity, have had their minds fortified, and
> in the hour of imminent danger, have been preserved or res-
> cued. He who was determined to do good, but knew not how,
> has had the way pointed out to him, and been piloted when
> surrounded by rocks and quicksands, to the attainment of his
> object to do good (pp. 95–96).

The object of both the YMCA and the city mission movement
was to bless young men and make them a blessing. The rules were
simple: attendees must be ages fourteen to thirty-five; they were to
meet regularly under an experienced Christian president for mutual
improvement and benevolence. The Bible was their rule, there were
to be no political discussions, and they had to go to the slums and
help those who had more need than themselves. Many of the young
men worked, however, and didn't have much time. Some ministers
also saw the great need in the slums and would visit for awhile, but
soon their other duties would come first.

David wrote:

> We proposed that one or more persons be set apart to the
> work of visiting the poor in their own dwellings, but party feel-
> ing ran so high that one would say he would give if the mission-
> ary or agent was from his denomination, another said if he was
> from his. . . . Finally it was agreed to try! . . . Laws were drawn

up to embrace the whole city on such a broad basis as to admit all evangelicals. . . . On January 1, 1826, the first City Mission was formed in Glasgow, Scotland (pp. 136–37).

Soon Miss Frances Hartridge took an interest in the mission and in David. Frances may have been one of the women who helped raise money for the first city mission. She probably helped address the two thousand letters describing a plan for city missions. The mailings went to Scotland, England, Ireland, France, other places on the continent of Europe, Asia, Africa, and America (p. 137).

What did she see in David—a sickly, lowly clerk-secretary for twenty-three societies? Yes, he was friends with the religious leaders of the city, the powerful, and the wealthy. She may have known that kind of man before, but here was a man, a real man, one who could win her heart. David was also a friend to young men in prison. He would sit with them all night and tell them of the Savior and then had the courage to be their Christian friend and stand by their side when they were hung. When David Nasmith walked the city's slum streets, prostitutes, thieves, and the most wretched of the poor knew him by name. Children who lived in the alleys ran up and grabbed him by the hand. David took the little ones up in his arms as they giggled and laughed. He smelled from picking up the odor of the slums, but Frances Hartridge must have thought, *Now there is a man, a man worth marriage, who could be a good father.* Sometimes David seemed to be proud and arrogant, but to Frances he was more humble than he appeared. He was bold and courageous, but most of all he loved the Lord and others. The poor of the city seemed to have all of his heart. Was there room for her?

Frances, whose family lived in England, was independent, and she was a businesswoman. Would she give all that up for him? In March 1828, David and Frances were married.

Few matches have been more equal, and seldom has more depended on such equality. . . . She was truly a helpmate to her husband, with a heart as large and a zeal as ardent as David had himself. . . . Her Christian virtue and moral courage did not fail (p. 138).

They helped each other in their spiritual walk, much like Jonathan Edwards, colonial theologian and evangelist, and his helpmate (p. 198). They found time together for prayer, encouragement, and hymn singing. As Adam needed help, so did David. The union of David and Frances became the miracle of marriage as God designed it to be when two become one, yet remain distinctive from each other. It is a mystery much like the Trinity and the very essence of it is the same love. They shared all the accomplishments and likewise all the pain—two separate people, yet one.

Shortly after their marriage, Frances went to England and David wrote to her:

> We have a hard time paying our bills, . . . the laborer is worth his hire! Surely the Lord will provide another situation for us. Business being too much for you I know your mind already. Let us cast all our care on the Lord, never forgetting what great things he has done for us (pp. 140–41).

After six years of working for the Institutional House and only one year of marriage, David resigned. David and Frances chose to live by faith, and David was to be a "general moral agent," an appropriate title for someone out to bring about moral change in the cities (p. 214).

The whirlwind of the marriage of David and Frances Nasmith picks up with such speed and touches down at so many different points of the world, it is hard to comprehend. Firmly hanging on to each other and hanging on to the Lord, led by the Spirit, they started city missions and young men's societies and associations all over the world.

Like Wesley and many other reformers, the Nasmiths' main support came from women. David wrote to a Miss Oswald:

> We meet with less opposition than I thought we would . . . Lee, our first agent sleeps on our couch. . . . Never have I been more truly happy than during the last months in our two rooms and kitchen. Mrs. Nasmith and I are, thanks be to God, of kindred spirits and this adds greatly to my happiness. Thank you for your gift. It is so much better for us not to take money from these people (pp. 176–77).

David records a momentous event in his journal, October 20, 1829, the birth of their first son, David.

> The Lord has in great kindness, granted to Mrs. Nasmith safe delivery of a son, today at half-past eleven o'clock. The boy is from the Lord, and we give him to be His. May his name be written in the lamb's book of life! May it soon appear that he is a vessel to show forth the praises of the Lord and to serve Him on the earth! His hair is like his mother's.

He is worthy of an English mother, a Scotch father, and an Irish birth-place.

The rescue ministry continued to rely on women.

> There are not less than 300 girl prostitutes in the town. Several have want to abandon their sinful place, but we could find no place for all of them. So we have rented some rooms and hired a woman to minister to them. . . . Many are opposed on the grounds that their cases are hopeless, but we know in whose hands are the hearts of all, and draw our confidence from the Scripture, that we shall not labor in vain. . . . One is a daughter of a minister (p. 196–200).

Frances and David returned home to Scotland for a little visit with family and friends. How happy Grandma Nasmith must have been to see her little grandson and listen to both Frances and David talk of things of the Lord. Was this not her prayer from the time David was born, that he would serve Jesus? Happy, yes, but nonetheless her heart breaks when she says good-bye to her grandchild—so little time together. Yet she knew God held them all, yes, even held the world in His hands.

Frances and David sold their furniture so they could go to America. The long voyage took courage for Frances as she looked over the wide blue ocean, no land in sight, rocking little David in her arms. She knew that she and David had put their hurts in the hands of God so that they could help others. She knew she had married a man with a vision and she shared that vision, but what lay ahead? The fear of the unknown would creep into her heart, and then the Lord would whisper, "Peace, be still," as the waves splashed against the ship.

David and Frances arrived in New York and stayed in a cheap boardinghouse for a while. Then David started traveling. Sometimes he took little David and Frances with him. They traveled by riverboat, canal boat, carriage, and the mail. It was a miracle of God that they could get evangelical Christians together from different denominations, sit them down—both men and women—tell them of the conditions of their cities and towns, and not be judgmental of those who lived within the moral decay, but proclaim, "I was chief of sinners, but by the grace of God go I!" They would set aside what divided them and come together for one purpose: fulfilling what the Scriptures told them to do about the poor. This was and is basic Christianity. "Religion that God our Father accepts as pure and faultless is this: to look after orphans and widows in their distress" (James 1:27).

With the constitution for the new mission complete and with the forms properly filled out—the name of the city, the names of the committee members (the Nasmiths' names appeared nowhere on the documents, for they believed the mission was the responsibility of the Christians in their own city)—they sometimes would close with the singing of a hymn:

Come, thou fount of blessing, Tune my heart to sing Thy grace;
Streams of mercy, never ceasing, Call for songs of loudest praise.
Teach me some melodious sonnet, Sung by flaming tongues above;
Praise the mount! I'm fixed upon it, Mount of Thy redeeming love.
Here I raise my sign of victory, Hither by Thy help I'm come.
And I know by Thy good pleasure, Safely to arrive at home.
Jesus sought me when a stranger, Wandering from the fold of God;
He, to rescue me from danger, Interposed His precious blood.
                                                          —Robert Robinson

David often was by himself, and if he had to stay in an inn, he tried to find a temperance inn and lodged with others in the travelers' room. He also stayed with the Native Americans, who, he said, were "very hospitable." He was gone sometimes for long periods, but he wrote to Frances often, and sometimes the letters would not come until he was home and gone again. Frances was a part of the ministry, a big part, and he needed her not only to come home to but to be part of him each day. The miracle is that the Spirit bridged this gap in miles, for when the words were not there on paper they were spoken to each others' hearts by the Spirit.

From Boston he wrote,

This is a most important city because of the mighty influence which it is capable of wielding over the New England States and the example which it may set to the whole of America and the world at large. I have never met with more valuable material and a spirit that is here for the advancement of the Lord's work. . . . the walls of party are high. What they spoke of as impossible, I know to be possible, and I hope that they may be led to find the truth of my statements ere long, by taking the course which will prove that it is possible for Baptists and Congregationalists to work together.

David's letters to Frances were about everything—the prisoners, the children at the Sabbath schools, prostitutes, everyone. They also contained a record of the religious leaders of the day, the conditions of travel, and the conditions of people. America, 1831: Jackson was president, the Civil War was thirty years away, the War of 1812 was over, and U.S. territory was expanded to the west. There were slavery disputes, tariff questions, new political parties, and the rise of humanitarian, educational societies, and movements. Feeling the heartbeat of compassion, David wrote:

> Visited infant school No. 1, visited in the company of an aged lady houses of bad fame . . . state prison . . . addressed 1,200 persons of color . . . Poor's House saw a number of mournful and interesting cases . . . visited a cave of a half-witted man, the poor man looked up, I could not help but think of Joseph. . . . Gave away a copy of Mrs. Bethune's Bible alphabet (always had tracts with) . . . A fellow passenger is on his way to introduce a new patent light made of alcohol as a substitute for oil. . . . talked of 1 Timothy 1:15, Christ Jesus came into the world to save sinners; of whom I am chief . . . shocked at the conditions of the poor Choctaw Indians . . . addressed the seamen . . . visited a sick man and three murderers . . . addressed 150 persons of color and the same day about 800 whites . . . Young men are dying off in groups from profligacy (dissipation, excessive drinking—licentiousness disregarding sexual restraints) and neglect during sickness. . . . slaves here are sold for $300 to $500, how painful the thought that fellow immortals should be bought and sold like bullocks! Slavery is a great curse on this land . . . addressed Sunday school . . . Many of the colored people are pious; in Savannah, 1,000 member church, another 2,014 . . . visited the Magdalene Asylum . . . I left in each city as I passed along a copy of the constitution of the New York City Mission. . . . I have been privileged to sound the alarm, and call the Lord's host to battle. . . . The poor Irish laborers perish in immense numbers. . . . Arrived in Princeton, heard Dr. Alexander preach a soul refreshing sermon from if I be lifted up will draw all men unto me . . . heard a sermon on temperance . . . When in secret prayer, I always feel pleasure more or less; why am I so seldom there? I take you and David with me [in prayer].

We can be sure that Frances took David into her prayers also and taught little David to do the same.

When he came home there was the time to refresh his clothes; he was a gentleman and felt that to meet with the leaders he had to dress that way. David and Frances felt that while they were wandering America they were like the children of Israel in the wilderness, their clothes did not wear out and they always had food. Church was always an important part of their lives. They were the kind that if it is open they will go. Their times together were most refreshing as they prayed before the Lord.

> I [we] have gone from shore to shore, from town to town, from country to country . . . counting nothing too dear to part with, no suffering too great to endure, to meet the people and urge them on to action in thy holy cause; and how has thou been with me; a mouth and wisdom thou hast been to me, my provider! My Corrector! (pp. 264–65).

David gave Frances a choice of living in New York, Paris, or London. God directed both of their hearts toward London at the same time.

In 1844 Dr. Campbell writes,

> In the states he has been instrumental in forming sixteen city missions; the American Young Men's Society and eight or ten auxiliaries to it; to which must be added, several associations in behalf of colored people, and also various benevolent associations for supplying the temporal wants of the poor. In Canada they formed fifteen societies. The moral influence he exerted on a multitude of the moving and leading people of the Christian Church, when you calculate the sum of this influence, who can estimate the affects which may flow from it for centuries to come? (pp. 260–61).

Upon their return to Europe, Frances's health deteriorated and she almost died. They were in Scotland (perhaps they lived with David's parents) and still believed they should go to London, but they had no money. These were hard years, and David traveled for another society in order to send money home. He was still starting city missions on the continent of Europe. At one time the people of France thought he was a spy.

David wrote to Frances:

> Time is passing. We have now been more than eight years traveling together. You have had much to bear with me; and it may be that I have had somewhat to bear with you. May we

this night be enabled mutually to forgive each other, and may we be forgiven in heaven! I believe we are forgiven. . . . Pray for me my dear; do bear up the hands of your affectionate husband. Does he not love you? God knows. Has he appeared in some of his moments as if he did not regard you sufficiently? Do suspend your judgment. You have been altogether ignorant of the struggles he has had when you little thought of it; when from a conviction that the Lord was with him, directing and blessing him in his attempts to serve his Master and your Master, he was led sometimes to do what he saw was acquiesced in rather reluctantly by his beloved partner. I know you have suffered privations not a few since you became my wife, (I trust for Christ's sake) which he knows, which in as far as they have been borne willingly, will not be forgotten by him. I have made several changes, but only when they seemed called for. If it is his will, I shall be glad, for your sake, that in future they be few (pp. 291–92).

Miss Read of Ireland gave a large sum of money and formed a group to support the London cause, enabling the start of a new mission. It may be that Frances was done nursing their youngest infant and had come into the living room and gently laid her down in a cradle next to David. David may have rocked the cradle with his foot, and the series of circumstances inspired his writing:

In a room of their little house in Canning-Terrace . . . on May 16, 1835, . . . a few men after prayer formed the London City Mission, adopted the constitution, assigned offices to each other; and after laying the infant Mission before the Lord, desiring that he would nurse and bless it, and make it a blessing to tens of thousands, we adjourned (pp. 310–11).

Thomas E. Buxton, M.P., who had given speeches in Parliament for the emancipation of the slaves, became the treasurer of the London mission and contributions started to flow in. Charles Dickens was gathering material for his books in the same neighborhoods where the first city missionary was sent. "With no theological training he set off for the filthy alleys and stinking court yards with their pimps and prostitutes, burglars and thieves, the Fagins and the Bill Sykeses so vividly depicted in *Oliver Twist*," wrote Phyllis Thompson. Here is the true spirit of Christmas 365 days a year! The London of Charles Dickens and of Frances and David Nasmith was not first and foremost red velvet coats and sleigh bells. There was poverty and suffering. Today, it still takes courage to walk down those alleys, and the spirit of Christmas lives on 170 years later in city missions all over the world. What evangelical Christians can do with love and compassion!

Frances was alone a lot while David was starting many new city and town missions, Young Men's Associations, Adult School Societies. The projects she probably helped on the most were the Female Rescue Mission; the London Female Mission, which included a rescue mission for prostitutes called the Female Friends Society; Maternal, Young Women and Little Girls Associations; Female and Family Missions; and Society for the Benefit of Domestic Servants. The object of the projects "was to improve the character and condition of young women. It seeks to reform the vicious to reclaim the wandering and to help and befriend the defenseless and the poor" (p. 351).

Criticism started to rise from the board and donations were down, causing David to resign as the free secretary of the London City Mission and form the British and Foreign Missionary Society. These were the hardest times of all for Frances. They had five children and little money. David, at the time, was often in depression. Frances wrote:

> David left on the train to go and start yet another City Mission. He got sick and was taken to an Inn, the disease was rapid and extensive, the surgeon applied 24 leeches to his stomach. . . . He laid still in the bed for awhile and then said, "I am ready to go whenever my Master calls me. There is nothing like being employed in his service. . . . I want you to have a City Mission here." . . . They came to get me but it was too late when I arrived (pp. 414–42).

David, forty years old when he died, left Frances an impoverished widow with five children.

David's body was brought to London and the corpse, followed by about thirty friends and all of the agents of the London City Mission, was taken into the Wesleyan Chapel, which was kindly lent for the occasion. After the funeral service, the hearse was followed by six mourning coaches, which went in procession to Bunhill Fields. The third hymn in the second book of Dr. Watts was read by the Rev. P. Lorimer of the Scottish Presbyterian Church, and 1 Corinthians 15 was read by the Rev. R. Philip of Marberly Independent Chapel, who delivered an address. They all sang:

> Christians and brethren, ere we part.
> Join every voice and every heart.

One solemn song to God we raise.
One final hymn of grateful praise.

On reaching the ground, the procession was met by the Rev. Peter Hall, who read the burial service of the Church of England. A widow fund was established for Frances and her children (p. 427).

The bitter and the sweet! Informed of the generosity of the people and their support of her and her five children, the widow Nasmith rejoiced, thanking the Lord that they would have food and a roof over their heads. A feeling of relief and gratitude must have swept over her for the sweet, wonderful thing they had done out of concern, out of love—but, oh, how bitter at times it must have seemed, when she rolled over in her cold bed at night never to feel the warmth of her David beside her again. He used to be gone for long periods of time, but she always knew he would be coming home, filled with wonderful stories, basking in the tenderness and joy of her and the children's company.

If our associates had only given support while he was still alive, she may have thought, *maybe he would still be alive*. They speak so well of him now, but when he was alive they could not push him into their mold and now he is no longer here. Now they give! How much more we could have done with this money!

Bitterness slipped into her mind and almost into her heart. But no! Frances knew the presence of her Savior as her mind filled with the comfort that David, free from pain, was with his Lord. How many times after his death did she read this old letter from David?

Yes, beloved, when we have put off this mortal, which will not be long with either of us, and meet with our dear children in heaven, what shall be our estimate of these light afflictions, when we shall see a James, a John, and we know not how many more, it may be some hundreds or thousands . . . with their palms of victory and crowns of glory, uniting with the ransomed throng in praising the Lamb, and are that these are the fruits of those missions in Scotland, Ireland, Canada, the United States, or France, that the Divine Redeemer told David Nasmith to take up his cross and go and establish. Shall we not in that day hide our heads, and regret that murmur was ever felt for any moment in our hearts, or escaped our lips, at parting with our little all, and suffering some few privations, seeing that such were some of the fruit? Would we not rather wish that we had ten thousand such privations to endure, if but one soul more had thereby been RESCUED

from Hell and conducted to Heaven? Let us beloved, live for
eternity; live for Jesus who died for us. I think I hear our
Lord say to us: "Fear not, be faithful unto death, and I will
give thee a crown of life." Difficulties and darkness may continue for a season, but an hour of deliverance will come. Yes
it will . . . be patient, be of good courage. He will strengthen
thee; yea, He will uphold thee! (pp. 292–93).

Conclusion

In 1844 Dr. Campbell asked, "What are the results of David and
Frances's American trip?" In 1994, the banquet hall was full. What a
mixture of people: Methodist, Presbyterian, Pentecostal, Baptist,
charismatic, noncharismatic, Democrats, Republicans, Hispanic,
Latino, black, white. We were sitting next to a young woman who
had been a prostitute. The testimonies rang out through the hall.
One young man said how he had been a drug user and pusher but
"now, Hallelujah! I'm 'clean' because of Jesus." As the words hit our
ears some of us had tears in our eyes and words on our lips, But for
the grace of God there go I."

Steve Burger, Executive Director of the International Union of
Gospel Missions, gave the opening remarks.

> Although this city is highly favored with religious privi-
> leges yet there are thousands who know as little of the Gos-
> pel as if it never had been preached in their land; . . . they are
> living as careless as if they were never to be called to account.
> There are thousands of families where the name of God is
> never mentioned except when it is taken in vain . . . a vast
> number of the poor have never been taught to read.

Steve paused, then looked up from the paper he had just read and
said, "That was taken from the first City Mission Report, January 1,
1827." The city missionaries gasped as we looked around at each
other; it sounded just like the people we work with today in our city.
My husband talked about how some things change and some things
don't. Now we are stressing education. Today the cutting-edge ministry is individualized computer learning centers. How can anyone
read the Bible or get a job without being able to read? More women
and children are homeless, there is more violence. How do we minister to diseases of the body and soul, to the elderly, to the mentally
ill? Steve closed with this:

> You will convert the houses that were tenanted by men of

the foulest passions into churches of the Redeemer where the Lord, the spirit will dwell, and where the God of salvation will be loved and served. You will arrest the progress of vice, and promote the interests of virtue; and you will make our poor, our degraded population stand forth in all that freshness and fairness of moral and of spiritual excellence.

He was reading again and said that also is from the first City Mission report, 1827—another gasp, for it, also, is true today. In that report are biblical principles and the how-to-do-it plan of city missions. The committee is now a board of directors. Twenty-nine thousand homeless people will sleep in rescue missions tonight. Now there are urban youth centers and we convert crack houses into youth centers.

We are continuing the heritage of David and Frances, in the power of the Holy Spirit, in the truth of the Scriptures. In the love of God we have put aside our cultural differences, our economic differences, our governmental differences, our church denominational differences, and we link our arms together reaching the cities for Christ. "But by the grace of God there go I." David and Frances were crazy, off the charts, out of the norm. That kind of love for the perverted, the suffering, the hurting, the lost, and the poor of the city? Change the city? You must be crazy! Yet Jesus wept over the city and went to the cross. The Nasmiths also wept over cities. Tears of love are one thing, but they also lived lives of love, compassion, commitment, and courage.

> This is how we know what love is: Jesus Christ laid down his life for us . . . let us not love with words or tongue but with actions and in truth" (1 John 3:16, 18).

> Love must be sincere. Hate what is evil; cling to what is good. . . . Do not be overcome by evil, but overcome evil with good (Romans 12:9, 21).

Bibliography

Shedd, Clarence Prouty, et. al. *History of the World's Alliance of Young Men's Christian Association* (London: S.P.C.K., 1955).
Dictionary of National Biography. Vol. 14. (London: Oxford University Press, 1964).

Additional Reading

Rare Books

Lectures Delivered Before the Young Men's Christian Association 1845–1846. Vol. 1. (James Nisbet & Co., 1875). Found at Babson Library, Springfield College, Springfield, Massachusetts.

A. G. Gallant. *Saint Mungo's Bells; or Old Glasgow Stories Rung Out Anew.* (David Bryce & Son, 1888). Found in the Mitchell Library in Glasgow, Scotland.

First Annual Report Glasgow City Mission (1827). Found in Mitchell Library, Glasgow.

The Note Book. Vol. 1. "Christian Work Among Young Men in Canada." (Toronto, Ontario YMCA). Found at Springfield College.

Current Books

Phyllis Thompson, *To the Heart of the City* (London: Hodder and Stoughton, 1985).

Edwin R. Orton, *Into the City: The Challenge of Urban Mission* (London: Birmingham City Mission, 1991).

June Owen, *The Heart of the City* (Australia: Kangaroo Press, 1987).

2

Out of the Miry Clay

Jerry & Maria McAuley

The well-beloved and loving wife and true helpmeet, who faithfully labored side by side with Jerry, sharing all the trials and triumphs of his redeemed life, and who bravely took up his work where he laid it down when the Lord called him home.

—*R. M. Offord* [1]

Introduction

*T*he "posse" sat there tan, good-looking, young, smug high
school students telling of their sexual adventures, how they
would "hit on a girl, have sex with her one after another while the
others watched. That's what the girls want; when the 'posse' chooses
a girl, it is a great honor for her."

That was horrible! But the appetite of the American people to see
these young men over and over again as they became the hot topic
for TV shows made me wonder, "Do we still live in a civilized country?" As we watched one of our favorite news shows, the usual stories
of war, crime, and health care marched across the screen. Then three
very young girls came on to tell of their sexual adventures. Equal
time, I guess. They all said they had done "it" at a young age—"If
you want friends, you just have to, everyone was doing it," and so on.
They told how most of the time they don't want to, nor did they
enjoy it, but because of their reputation, now the guys expected it.
They were trapped. By the end of the interview, each girl said she
wished she was still a virgin, but that she would probably get pregnant, be a single mom, and that there was *no hope!*

What about the girl, the woman, who boldly sells her body? Is
there hope for her? Or the woman who has been married one, two,
three times, looking for love but getting beaten up and having kids
one after another? Is there hope for her? Sexual immorality is ram-
pant, yet there is hope, praise God! Each individual can be rescued,
can find the love he or she needs and is looking for. Hope! Hope is
found in the Holy Bible. I believe the greatest heroine for these girls—
women—is found in Mary Magdalene. She was last at the cross and
first to see the risen Savior. He had protected her, rescued her from
sin, and given her a life of real love.

Maria Fahy was a nineteenth-century Mary Magdalene. She had
run away from home to the streets of New York City and had become
a "fallen woman" who lived with a man named Jerry McAuley. Both
were rescued, and they established the first rescue mission founded
by individuals who had been lifted up out of the miry clay.

❧❦❧

Like so many girls today, Maria Fahy's childhood was one of heartbreak, poverty, fear, and loneliness. When she was young, her mother
died, her father disappeared, and she had to earn her own living. So,
like thousands of others in the 1800s looking for opportunity, looking for a job, New York City was her destination.[2] As she headed
down the dusty country roads, there was a hope in her heart that
things would be better. To pass the time, she probably sang some of

the Sunday school songs she had learned. But New York City was on her mind, all the stories she had heard of it, and now she was on her way, leaving the past and its misery behind.

When Maria arrived, she was overwhelmed by the excitement, the crowds of people, and the kinds of activities around her. She looked for a job here and there, but there was none for her, and soon she found herself in a part of town that was even more exciting. There was talk on the streets of the "rat pit," where dogs were trained to kill rats, and if that became boring, a young man would jump into the pit, pick up a rat with his teeth, and chew it to death. Maria's stomach turned at the thought, but still the excitement of the idea that someone would do that worked in her mind. Then there was the saloon that had the "wickedest man in New York." He had a son only two years old who lived in the saloon with him. The father had the son perform to the amusement of the adults by asking him questions, and he would spit out the answers like a little toy soldier. His dad would ask, "What state do you live in?" "New York State." "What country?" "United States." "Who's the president of the United States?" "Lincoln." "What'll you do when you get to be a man?" "Marry." "What'll you do to your wife when you marry her?" "Mash her head." The crowd would roar with laughter. This, too, made Maria uncomfortable, but she was still intrigued by it.

It started to get dark as she walked down the streets; the loud, gay music came out of the saloons and brothels. She looked in and her eyes seemed to jump out of her head at the glitter, at the women in silk and satin. She stood in her drab, old worn clothes as her stomach started to growl from lack of food. That night she found a little place behind a building where she curled up and went to sleep. *It isn't so bad*, she thought. *After all, I've been in worse situations before. Tomorrow I'll find a job*, she promised herself. When she awoke, she was hungry, but that wasn't new, either. Brushing herself off, she went back onto the streets with the great courage of youth. How long did it take for courage to turn into discouragement? No one knows.

Being hungry is what finally made Maria slip. A man said he would buy her some food, for which she was very grateful, and when she was finished, he took her to buy beautiful clothes. First she had a bath, and that felt so good. Then she put on her beautiful dress, and while looking in the mirror, she twirled around and she thought, *Now I'm really somebody*. Maria was pretty and she knew it. Soon she was the center attraction in the saloon hall. All the men's eyes turned to her when she entered. The madam said, as she put her arm around her, "I will take care of you, Maria, like all my girls, and you can stay here." It was like one giant party and it was fun. Her first drink was bitter, but soon she loved drinking, which made her less aware of the activities that went on in the little private booths when men took her upstairs. The life of a prostitute lasted only about five years, and Maria's life was quickly slipping away. Soon her thirst for liquor made her into a drunk, no longer beautiful and youthful. She found herself in the basements of the saloons and the subcellars where the most despicable acts of perversion took place.

We don't know when Maria met Jerry McAuley, but she became Jerry's girl, and that gave her a feeling of belonging. They were both living on the wild side, the fast lane, in the pit of despair and grime. The slimy mud of sin had them stuck in a life that was choking them to death as they sunk deeper.

Jerry describes his life and their life together and shows us how God developed a powerful love—compassion that not only reformed them, but thousands like them, like you and me. But for the grace of God there go I.

Me father was a counterfeiter and ran away from justice before I can remember him. There was a lot of us, and they put me with my grandmother. I would throw things at her just to hear her curse and swear and then she would hit the floor praying on her knees. I got well beyond her or anybody by the time I was thirteen. They let me run loose. I had no schooling and got beat for food and drink till I wished my self dead many a time. I thought if I could only get to my sister in America it would be Paradise and when I got there I helped my brother-in-law for a while. I was tall for my age and strong, and had no fear for any man living, a born thief, stealing came natural and easy, soon I was in a den on Water Street learning to be a prize-fighter and with a boat on the river for stealing at night. I made good hauls for the river police didn't amount to much in them days, and it was easy. By this time I was nineteen and I suppose there wasn't a bigger nuisance or loafer. Now I'd enough to send me to prison forty times over, and I knew it, but that didn't make it any easier to go there for something I hadn't done. A crime was sworn on me by some that hated me bad and wanted me out of the way. Fifteen years in prison, that was the sentence I got, and I was not twenty years old. That hour going up the river was the toughest I'd ever come to. . . . I was mad with rage and wanted to kill the guard.[3] And when I put on the prison clothes and they shut me in, I knocked my head against the wall, and if I dared I would have killed myself. At last I made up my mind I'd obey the rules, an see if I could get pardoned out, or maybe there would come a chance of escape. I set me mind toward that.

I tried it for two years; learned to read, and had a pile of cheap novels they let us buy; an I learned carpet weaving an no one had a word to say against me. But then I grew weak, I'd been use to open air always, and a shut in life was hard on me. Then I got ugly and thought it was no use, an they punished me. Do you know what that is? It's the leather collar that hold and galls you strapped up by the arms with your toes just touching the floor, an its the shower bath that leaves you in a dead faint till another dash brings you out. I've stood it all and cursed God while I did. I was that desperate I would have killed the guard, but I saw no chance out even if I did.

It was one Sunday morning. I'd been in prison five years. I dragged me self into the chapel and sat down; then I heard a voice I knew and looked up. There by the chaplain was a man I'd been on a spree with many a time—Orville Gardner. He stepped down off the platform. "My men," says he, "I have no right anywhere but among you, for I have been one of you in sin," and then he prayed till there wasn't a dry eye there but mine; I was that shamed to be seen crying, but I looked at him and wondered what had come to make him so different. He said a verse that struck me an when I got to me cell again I took down the Bible and began to hunt for it. I read it for a while . . . and I pitched me Bible down and kicked it all around the cell.[4]

. . . I wanted to be different. I thought about the new look in Gardner's face. "What makes it?" says I, "an he's different, why can't I be?" . . . You wouldn't think I'd minded, but if ten thousand people had been in my cell, I couldn't a felt worse about praying. I knelt down blushing that hot as I'd never done in me life before, an then I'd up again, and that's the way it was for three or four weeks, till I was just desperate. Then there comes a night when I said I'd pray till some sense comes to me, and if it didn't I'd never pray again. I was that weak and trembly it seemed as if I could die easy enough. I knelt there and waited between the times I prayed. I wouldn't stir from my knees. My eyes were shut. I was in agony, and the sweat rolling from my face in big drops and "God be merciful to me a sinner" came from my lips. Then in a minute, some thing seemed to be by me. I heard a voice, or I felt I heard one plain enough. It said, "My son, thy sins which are many, are forgiven." I think I saw a light about me, and smelled something as sweet as flowers in the cell. I didn't know if I was alive or not. I shouted out, "Oh praise God! Praise God!" "Shut your noise," the guard said, going by. "What's the matter with you?" "I've found Christ," I says, "Me sins are all forgiven me." "I'll report you." Says he, and he took me number, but he didn't report me.

Well, then, seeing how it had come to me, I began to pray for others. I was quiet and content all the time. I believe it was good for me, God did find a way to let me out of prison. I didn't pray for it for two years, but just worked there to save others, and many a one turned to a new life and stuck to it. Then at last came a pardon when I'd been in seven years and six months, and I come back down the river to New York. There was never a more lonely man a live. I wouldn't go back to my old neighborhood for fear I would be tempted and so I wandered around trying to find work, till one day I found a friend and he took me to a lager beer saloon. Lager beer had come up since I went up the river. I didn't know it was any more hurt than root beer, but that first night did for me. Me head got in a buzz, and in a week or two I wanted something stronger. I got work in a hat shop, and had good wages, but a strike come and I led it and lost my job.[5]

Probably by this time Maria was Jerry's girl, Nellie was Tom's girl, and Tom was Jerry's partner.[6] They all lived together, drank heavy together, and spent money together on whatever they wanted. Maria was a waitress-entertainer in one of the variety houses. While other men were fighting in the Civil War, and women were trying to keep the home fires burning, these four were living off the war in such an evil way that Satan himself must have been pleased. Jerry continues,

It was war time, and I went into the bounty business—a rascally business, too. Then I had a boat on the river again. I'd buy stolen goods off the sailors, and then make them en-list for fear of being arrested and I took the bounty. The end of the war stopped this an then I stick to the river buyin' an sellin' smuggled goods and payin' all I could in counterfeit money. Do you remember when the Idaho burned in the East River? Me and my partners rowed out, not to save life, but to rob; but when we saw them screaming in the water we

turned and helped them, though one of my partners in the
boat said we could of made a pile pickin' up coats and hats.
Often and often I was shot at. Do you think I didn't remember what I'd had given to me and how I had lost it? I didn't
pray, I didn't dare to, I kept under liquor all the time to head
off thinking for I said God was done with me, and I was bound
for hell sure and certain.

About this time, one night I'd gone over to Brooklyn, very
drunk, too drunk to do me share of the work we had laid out
for the night, and as me partner boarded the ship we were
after, I slipped and fell overboard and went under like a shot.[7]
. . . I knew I was drowning, for I went down twice, and with
only me hand stickin' out of the water, I called on God, though
I felt too mean to do it. It seemed as if I was lifted up and the
boat brought to me. I got hold of it some how. The water
had sobered me up. When I was in it, I heard, plain as if a
voice spoke to me, "Jerry, you've been saved for the last time.
Go out on that river again and you will never have another
chance."

I was mad. I went home and drank and drank and drank. I
was stupid with drink and as awful lookin' a case—more so
than you have ever laid eyes on. And oh the misery of me
thought. I was sick with remembering and yet drinking day
and night to drown it all.

A city missionary come in one day to the house. He stepped
back a bit when he saw me at the top of the stairs a head like
a mop and an old red shirt. He had been pitched down stairs
by fellers like me, and I had done it meself once. I hung around
while he went in a room, thinking maybe he could get me a
job of honest work, and when he came out I told him so. He
asked me to step out on the pavement. He said afterwards I
was that evil-looking, he was afraid of me and he didn't know
what I might do. So out on the street I went, and he took me
straight to the Howard Mission and there we had a long talk,
and a gentleman wanted me to sign the pledge. "It's no use"
says I; "I shall break it." "Ask God to keep you from breaking
it," he said. I thought a minute, and then I signed it and went
home. My partner was there, and he laughed himself hoarse
when I told him. He had a bottle of gin in his hand that very
minute. "You!" he says; "here, drink!" I took the glass and
drank. "That's the last glass I'll ever take," says I. "Yes," says
he, "Till the next one." I had hardly swallowed it, when who
should come in, but the missionary. We went out together;

and I told him I was dead broke and hungry, and I would
have to go to the river once more, anyhow. "Jerry," says he,
"before you shall ever do that again, I'll take off this coat and
pawn it." The coat was thin and old. I knew he was poor, and
it went to me heart that he'd do such a thing as that. He went
away a minute, and when he came back he brought me fifty
cents.[3]

The next day, Henry Little and two women city missionaries visited Jerry and Maria. Some described that part of New York City as
the wickedest place on earth. What took place in the late 1800s is no
different from what takes place today in the late 1900s. Evil is evil
and Satan does not change, whether it is behind closed doors, out in
the open, or on TV. Evil did not stop the city missionaries. They had
love, they had compassion, they had courage.

Jerry said, "Little kept on helping, he followed me up day after
day." One day he invited Jerry and Maria to his home, not far away,
where he lived with Mr. and Mrs. Franklin Smith. After they ate and
had tea, they read some Scripture, sang a hymn or two, and it was
time for prayer. They all got down on their knees. Mrs. Smith, a city
missionary, prayed. Jerry thought his knees would bust and later he
said, "I looked through my fingers to see if she was ready to quit.
Her pleading face was turned to Heaven, tears streaming from her
eyes as she was talking to Jesus about me, and I thought 'Oh, that
woman loves my soul.'"[9]

"Pray for yourself and God will save you." "I don't know
how," I said; "I can't put the words together." It wasn't that I
had forgotten all about praying; but after I had sinned so
fearfully, I felt afraid to utter such solemn words. "Pray the
prayer of the publican," some one cried; "God be merciful to
me a sinner." I prayed it. My heart was all broken, and I repeated
the words over and over. "Put in for Jesus sake," said the
missionary. . . . "I am saved," I cried; "Jesus has saved me."[10]
I prayed myself once more, and believed I should be
forgiven. There wasn't any shouting this time, but there
was quiet and peace. Little stayed close to me side and helped
me find jobs along the waterfront, but it wasn't easy me a
ex-con.

Maria and Jerry went with the city missionaries to services during
the week and on Sundays went to the Howard Mission and Home
for Little Wanderers. That mission took care of orphans and other

children whose families were having a hard time. Alfrederic Smith Hatch was a supporter of the mission, and he became a good friend. Jerry said of him, "He said I could always come and see him." He was a wealthy man and a powerful man and was one of the pioneers of the stock exchange.

Maria went to the meetings and heard the Gospel and the invitation, but it had no effect on her. She often said, "It sounded like another language." It did, however, make her think of her childhood days in Sunday school. The mission workers were kind to Maria.

When Jerry left his partner, Tom, he found Maria a place to live. One day Maria and Jerry came to the Howard Street Mission. Jerry asked Hatch, "What should we do because we are not married?" To Hatch the answer was simple—get married. But Maria was not sure at all. She was confused and to her, Jerry had gotten strange with all his talk about being saved. Hatch told them, "You should not live together." The advice was hard on Jerry, but he did want to do things right. It hurt Jerry when Maria left to live with a Christian family that his new friends found for her in New Jersey.

When Maria left the city, tears came to her eyes. She wondered if Jerry, the only one who ever had taken care of her, really cared about her. As she looked over her shoulder, she remembered her girlfriends and when they had lived in the subcellars. *No! No!* She thought. *I just can't go back to that.* Then she thought about the Christians she was sent to live with. *I'm a fallen woman,* she thought, *an outcast. Those religious church people will never accept me, but I promised I would try.*

Jerry added, "It wasn't long but I got lonely, so lonely for Maria. And soon I was on the stagecoach, I had to see her. We stopped at a bar and I had a drink and in a short time I was so drunk I wanted to kill myself. When I got back to New York City, I confessed about my drinking and asked people to pray for me. I had been out of prison for six years and it took another year by 1870 before I stopped the fallin' back to drink."

> It was a hard pull. I got work now an then, but more often not, and then everybody thought I was acting for what I could get out of it. I didn't wonder and helped it along by doing what you'd never believe, I caved in again. Three times I was drunk, and do you know what did it? Tobacco! That's why I'm down on tobacco now. Chew and smoke, there will be a steady craving for something and mostly it ends in whiskey. A man that honestly wants the Spirit of God in him has got to be clean, I tell you, inside and out. He's got to shut down on all his old dirty tricks, or he's gone. That's the way I found it.[11]

When Maria left the city her new friends hoped by leaving the places of temptation and living among good people, she would be brought to choose the right way. Here she was taught in religious things, attended family worship, and read the Bible, but still her heart was not reached.

Later God led her down east, and there alone, while asking prayer in a little Methodist church, God spoke and claimed all the glory. Suddenly the blessed truths of the Gospel were revealed to her. They came to her, just as knowledge seems to open to a little child, we don't know how, only we find when we are not looking for it that the child knows. Her blind eyes in an unexpected moment were touched, and she saw; her deaf ears were unstopped, and she heard. The way of salvation opened before her, and the words she had so often heard, that had slipped off from her like water from a rock were all at once full of life and power. They took hold of her conscience and heart; the lessons of her childhood came to her with a meaning they had never had, and she believed on the Lord Jesus Christ and was saved.

When Jesus was revealed to her she received him gladly, and gave herself wholly to Him. It was no halfway work with her. Her faith was childlike, her love simple and earnest. She at once received power to lift her out of the bondage of sinful appetite, and her soul was possessed with a love for sinners and a desire to lead others to the same precious Savior she had found. She could not rest day or night for the longing she had to tell the glad story of her salvation.

She came back to the city and commenced missionary work, in the employ of some Christian women, as a Bible reader in the Fourth Ward. She found easy access to tenement houses, liquor saloons, and dens of infamy, and in every place she testified of the grace of Christ and besought sinners to behold the Lamb of God who taketh away the sins of the world. Many listened, forsook their evil ways, and came to Jesus.[12]

In 1872 Jerry and Maria were married at the Howard Street Mission. Hatch was there, and by this time he had become vice president and director of the Chesapeake and Ohio Railroad. He was still a Wall Street banker. Jerry and Maria moved into an apartment on Division Street and their Christian friends came to visit often.

Continuing, in Jerry's words,

Maria has been God's help from that day to this, and often

we talked about some way to get at the poor souls in the fourth ward. We were doing a days work both of us, and poor as poor can be. But we said, "Why have we both been used to filth and nastiness, and all else, if not so as to know how to help some others out of it?" And one day I had sort of a vision; I thought we had a house in the fourth ward, and a stream of people coming in. I washed them outside and the Lord washed them inside; and I cried as I thought, "O, if I could only do that for Jesus' sake." "Do it for one if you can't do it for more," said Maria. And that's the way we begun, in an old dilapidated tenement of a house, in one room and a little sign hung out: The Helping Hand for Men. You would never believe how many that sign drew in. We did what we could, and when Thanksgiving Day came, friends gave us a good dinner for all. Afterwards there was a meeting and it was so blessed we were moved to say that they should come the next night. From that day till this—first in the old building, and then in this, the new one—there's been a meeting every night in the year, and now it's hundreds—yes thousands—that can say the Water Street Mission was their help to a new life.

Day and night we work—you know how. My life is slowly but surely going from me. I feel it, but living or dying it's the Lord's. All these years he has held me, but I don't know now but that I would have fallen again if I hadn't been so busy holding on to others. And that's the way to keep men—set them to work. The minute they say they are sick of the old ways, start them to pull in somebody else. You see when your soul is just on fire longing to get at every wretch and bring him into the fold, there is no time for your old tricks and no wanting to try them again. I could talk a month telling of one and another that's been here.[13] Oh, there's stories if one but knew them! And not a day but that you don't know there ain't a bummer in the area so low down but what the Lord can pick him out of the gutter and set him on his feet. That's why I tell me story and everything right out plain. There is times I'm sick of remembering it, but I have to do it, and them very times seems the ones that help the most. And as long as tongue can move, may I never be ashamed to tell what I have been saved from.[14]

Good and upright is the LORD; therefore will he teach sinners in the way (Psalms 25:8 KJV).

He is able also to save them to the uttermost that come unto God by him [Jesus], seeing he ever liveth to make intercession for them" (Hebrews 7:25 KJV).

I call to mind one instance, and relate it to show how we were led. One night we found the Mission without a cent, and forty odd tramps to feed and nothing to offer them. . . . I felt for these poor hungry men. Some of them had probably not tasted a bit of food for two and three days; they had no money to help themselves, and when they came on Saturday night we usually kept them over Sunday, but on this night we were broke.

We proceeded to the Mission-room and commenced the services, and some souls were saved. But even when nine o'clock had come, strange to say no one had handed us a penny. As the meeting drew to a close and nothing came, oh how dark everything looked; my faith trembled. I could hardly keep from crying as I looked into the hungry faces of my poor tramps and converts. I spoke to my wife about them, and she replied: "the Lord will provide; you see if he don't!"

I closed with a heavy heart and dismissed the meeting, and my wife took her position at the door, as usual, to shake hands with the folks as they went out. A lady passed out with her husband, and after going five or ten yards suddenly stopped, and coming back to my wife said, "Mrs. McAuley, we keep a baker-shop in Cherry Street, and I just happened to think you had better send up and get $5 worth of bread!" There was God's hand in answer to prayer, and we soon had enough for all and some to spare.[15]

About Maria, I am sure that my work would not be half so successful as it is without her. She is truly a helpmeet from the Lord to me. . . . I bless God that He permitted us to be united, and to work together in the Helping Hand; and I hope God will let us live a great while to labor for souls. We find it sweet to work for him, and though we know we are in ourselves very weak and helpless, and prone to mistakes, yet we trust in the Lord, and feel that his precious blood is applied every moment to cleanse and save us. Glory be to Jesus! (pp. 43–45).

I had been around New York some, and I thought I knew the worst places in it; but I was mistaken, for I'd never seen anything so bad as this neighborhood. The first time I found out what it was really like happened this way: There was a fellow they called Happy Joe came up one night and got a little full, and began to sing a hymn he'd heard down at our

Water Street place; and at last he said, "Let's have a Jerry McAuley prayer-meeting, right here!" Well, the girls jumped at the idea, and he took me off, and made fun of the whole thing. Well, sir, that blaspheming rascal was the cause of my coming here! Those girls were so interested from his description that two of them came down to Water Street in a carriage to our meetings, and then often came. One of them came to me afterwards and wanted me to help find her sister, who had got into some bad place up-town, she was afraid. Mrs. McAuley and I got interested, and we came up to look for the girl's sister. We started in at Bleecker Street, took in the Allen's, Harry Hill's, Wes Allen's, and all the rest there, and came up and went to nearly all the Sixth Avenue dives. Before we got through I made up my mind that this was a worse place than Water Street, and resolved, if the Lord would help me, to start a Mission up here. I finally fixed on this place, because it was about the worst I could find.

Maria McAuley says:

We felt that our work in Water Street was done and the time had come when we ought to make a change. After this visit it seemed to us that the cry went up to heaven for a mission here, that some of the hundreds of young men and women frequenting these dens and dives might be saved. We went home and prayed God if he wanted us up here to open the way; and if he didn't want us here to put up a barrier so high we couldn't climb over it. After many prayers and tears and with much fear and trembling, we found a place. The Cremorne McAuley Mission, 104 West 32nd Street, became a reality in January 1882 (pp. 109–10).

One night, after listening to the story of the woman of Samaria, Jerry said:

She was a hard case. Respectable women would have not associated with her; but the Son of God condescended to talk with her. She wanted Christ's gift so that she might no longer have the trouble of coming to the well to draw water. I was a brute, I was one of the worst devils ever let loose in society, but the glorious Gospel contained in that blessed Bible civilized me. It is the greatest civilizer in the world. There is no power like it. It made a man and a Christian and a good citizen of me (p. 132).

By this time Maria had been doing much of the work because Jerry had been sick for a long time with "consumption"—tuberculosis. His lungs were weak. He took his last breath with Maria at his side. Those were the days when people died at home. Often it took days— weeks—but there was time for prayers, singing, and reading the Word. They had been married twelve short years and Jerry was only forty- five when he died in September 1888.

> When Jerry died the trustees in charge of the Mission re- alized that a superintendent must be appointed in his stead. Many friends of the cause asked "Who can take his place?" To say that none could do so would be to limit the power of God to anoint souls for his work. The trustees felt that God had the agent ready, and so sought wisdom and direction from above. . . . From the very beginning of his mission- work Jerry had found a consecrated, cheerful, and able helper in the person of his wife. To her the sacred trust, the conduct of the Mission, was committed; and the Lord blessed her labors and those of the many faithful and devoted helpers who upheld her hands. With the same deep love and hunger for souls that characterized her husband, with never-failing tact, with much of Jerry's gift of keen penetration into hu- man nature, Mrs. McAuley labored to the utmost of her strength in her unremitting efforts to win the lost. She gave her testimony in the meetings, as she had always done, often with tears in her own eyes, and often bringing tears to the eyes of her listeners. She spoke frankly of her lost condition before Jesus saved her. It was a sad story; she did not glory in it: far from that—it was with a pang of grief and with a sense of humiliation that she told it. But she felt as Jerry ever felt, that poor souls, hearing how she was lifted from the depths and royally redeemed, would take heart, and be led to seek the same saving grace that she had found. And it was just in this way that her testimony and the testimonies of others, given in the Mission meetings, were blessed (p. 214).

Offord records testimony time at the mission:

> Many a time I have said to Jerry McAuley, "Mr. McAuley, I mean, by the grace of God, to keep in this way." He would say, "My boy, hold on to Christ." Now he has fought and won, but he is not out of sight altogether; I shall meet him again.

"I can praise God to-night. How I do praise him for answering my prayer for mercy ten months ago!" another said. Then we sang from the hymn—

> Let the lower lights be burning,
> Send a gleam across the wave,
> Some poor fainting, struggling seaman
> You may rescue, you may save
> —Philip P. Bliss

One convert said,

> That illustrates my case. . . . Until I came here, eighteen months ago, my wife and family were heart-broken. I was a drunkard, and when I came home my wife did not know whether to expect a kind word or a blow. This went on for eighteen years. . . . Rum had so much the best of me that I had lost my will. How many fights with the devil I had! Eighteen months ago I came here and was saved; now I am able to say "no" when tempted to do wrong.

"I thought I was as good as anybody until, as I came to this meeting, I discovered I was as bad as anybody," was the testimony of one who added, "I want to keep my light low that others may see it. My prayer is that God may keep me humble and honest" (p. 219).

Maria was the superintendent of the Cremorne McAuley Mission for eight years under an all-male board of trustees. Her health was poor and she finally persuaded the board to accept her resignation. There was a farewell service for Maria and here are some of the remarks.

In his comments, Alfred Hatch said,

> What would otherwise be the unmixed sadness of the parting is, however, turned into gladness by the blessed assurance that His power, His love, and the blessings of salvation through Jesus Christ will, while going with you, still remain with us.
>
> For nearly ten years you have faithfully and lovingly labored in this place for the salvation of sinners; and especially of those whose sins had plunged them in degradation so deep as to place them seemingly almost beyond the reach of human sympathy and help or of ordinary Christian influences.
>
> You and Jerry brought to the work in Cremorne Mission ten years ago the rich experience, the chastened spirit, the intimate knowledge of the heart-wants of sin-sick men and

women, the sublime faith in Jesus' love for sinners and His
willingness and power to deliver them from sin, and the ready
tact in turning their faltering footsteps heavenward with
which your own wonderful salvation and your ten preceding
years of earnest work in Water Street had endowed you.

When it pleased God to call Jerry home, you were
unhesitatingly chosen to take his place as Superintendent
of the Mission, a responsibility rarely before tendered to or
accepted by a woman alone. With a humble sense of your
own insufficiency, but animated and upheld by an unfaltering
trust in God, you took up the work where he had laid it
down, and took upon yourself the cares, the trials, the anxi-
eties and the burdens which you and he had previously borne
together.

To your fidelity and zeal, and the good judgment and tact
with which you have performed the laborious and often deli-
cate and perplexing duties imposed upon you, and avoided
the dissensions and jealousies by which Christian effort is so
often paralyzed, much of its continued prosperity and use-
fulness have, under God, been due. The devotion and single-
ness of purpose with which you have sought the salvation of
those whom the providence of God has brought within the
reach of your influence, claims no commendation less au-
thoritative than the final "Well done, good and faithful servant" of the Master Himself. The unfaltering courage with
which, in your personal testimonies, you have revealed the
darkness and sin which overshadowed your early life, in order that you might thus exalt the love and grace that drew
you out into the light and joy of His salvation, finds its highest vindication and its sweetest reward in the answering testimonies of multitudes who have been encouraged by the
story of your redemption to look to the Savior who saved
you. The encouragement and hope which these testimonies
have held out to despairing sinners, and the impulse which
has been given to the spirit of fearless testimony in others by
your example in this respect, faithfully continued after you
had attained a position in which motives of worldly policy or
personal pride, and sometimes the advice of well-meaning
friends, would have closed your lips and drawn the veil of
oblivion over the sinful past, must ever remain to you a sweet
compensation for all of personal feeling that they may have
cost you (pp. 231–33).

Offord added,

I am thankful, too, for all the inspiration she has been enabled to give to Christian workers. When I have sometimes felt
discouraged, she has helped me by her example, and her words
have encouraged me to take hope and have strengthened my
faith in work of this kind. I am personally grateful to her for all
the friendship I have enjoyed with her these many years, and
there are other hearts here that feel as I do. I do not know how
it was, but Mrs. McAuley could make you feel that, if she cared
for and sympathized with any one soul more than all the rest in
the world, you were just that one. This is a wonderful gift—
whether the gift of nature, or of grace, or of both. I have put the
sentiments of my heart and yours into verse, which I will read:

Farewell, dear friend? If lips must speak the word, Farewell!
Though with a pain of heart that lips can never tell;
We could have wished thy hands the work had ne'er laid down,
Until the call to wear the everlasting crown.
We praise our God to-day for all those hands have wrought,
For straying ones reclaimed, in love and pity sought;
For words of help, and hope, and winning tenderness,
That fell on weary souls to comfort and bless;
For tears o'er sinners shed, like summer's gentle rain;
For smiles that won the lost to God's dear love again;
For souls from sin's sad thrall so royally set free,
Through God's rich blessing on thy patient ministry.
Farewell, dear friend! Whate'er henceforth in life betide,
The Lord thy pilot be, 'mid changing scenes to guide,
To lead thee to that land whose bliss no tongue can tell,
Where partings are unknown, and none shall say farewell!
There waits thy crown, and richer far than all reward,
The sweet "Well done" and "Welcome." of thy loving Lord;
And there, in fulness, shall the harvest all be known,
The seed of which thy hands while here on earth have sown.

The Rev. John Calvin Knox, pastor of a church, said,

I sometimes get a little discouraged, and when I feel that
way I get right down on my knees at the side of my trunk and
get out two pictures; one is a picture of Jerry and the other of
Mrs. McAuley. I went into the Water Street over thirteen
years ago without God or hope in this world, and I thank

God I heard the invitation of Mrs. McAuley—"Come tomorrow night"—and took it. I can't say any more.

He was overcome with tears and took his seat. Maria McAuley
was then called upon to speak.

I cannot reply to all that has been said tonight. It is in my
heart; but I am slow of speech. I cannot say what I want to
say, but God knows that I feel it. In all these years that I have
been working here, I want to say publicly here before the
Board of Trustees, they have always stood by me, shoulder to
shoulder, in this work. I have always had their prayers and
their sympathies, and they have always had mine. I wish to
thank them to-night. I wish I could say what is in my heart. I
never could say "thank you" very gracefully, but when I say it
I mean it, and "thank you" from me means volumes.

When I spoke to one of the trustees, about eight or nine
months ago, and said I thought when I went away that Mr.
and Mrs. Ballou, of the Third Avenue Mission, would be good
Superintendents, he did not think they could be secured. He
did not know I had been praying to God to open up the way
for them, and when I sent for them and told them I was going to resign, it took their breath away. I asked them if they
would accept and they said, "We do not know what to say."
They came to the conclusion that they would ask God, and if
He wanted them they would come. . . . Finally they decided
to come; and I commit this work, first to God and His wonderful love, and then to their tender and loving care. And
now I want you to do something for me to-night those of
you who can, those of you who will. I want you to put up
your hands all those who will stand by Mr. and Mrs. Ballou.

Many hands were raised and Maria continued:

Oh, friends, I cannot tell what God has done for me. I
expect to tell my testimony while life shall last, if it will win a
precious soul for Jesus. I want to say that I was once a poor
homeless drunkard. I had no God and no hope, no home and
no friends; and I cried unto God and He heard my prayer,
and He put hope into my life. How I thank God for the way
He has brought everything round up to this night! You ask
me if I am not sorry I am going away. Do you not suppose
there is an ache in my heart? God knows there is—He knows

all about it. I am so glad to leave you in such good hands—such a Board of Trustees as there is in this Mission, who have stood by me through all the changing and trying times, man to man, and shoulder to shoulder. I want to thank them and my friends for the beautiful present they have given me, because I know it is a tribute of love, and it has cost them something to give toward that present. Soon after I came on the platform this evening I knew something was coming. I did not know what it was; but Trixie came to me and said, "Mrs. 'Cauley, I cannot sit beside you to-night." I said, "Why cannot you sit near me?" and she said, "I won't tell you," and she was so afraid she would tell me that she ran away.

Now I am going to tell you what I want to see to-night. I want to see some poor, tired, weary soul find rest—that is what I want more than all else. I am hungry for souls. God bless you—God bless you all. I can say no more.

In his book, Offord records that

A number of the converts and other friends of the Mission spoke briefly, and Mrs. McAuley followed in a touching prayer. At the conclusion of the service the usual "after-meeting for those desiring to lead a new life was held, Mrs. McAuley presiding for the last time, and uttering earnest words of help and sympathy, and leading one and another of the kneeling penitents to pray, "God be merciful to me a sinner, for Jesus' sake."

It was after midnight when the last good-bye had been spoken and the lights were turned out. Those who were present on this impressive occasion will never forget the scene. It was a happy, hearty testimonial to a faithful woman whom God has crowned with marvelous success as a soul-winner (pp. 236–41, edited).

Maria, in poor health, resigned as the superintendent of the mission but still lived her life with compassion, courage, commitment, and love. She probably still lived upstairs over the mission and could be often found ministering to people. Her life was entwined with the poor, the weak, the lonely, the rich, the powerful, and the famous.

If we are to understand the next chapter of her life, we must go back to the time when Jerry was still alive. By the 1800s, the McAuley Mission had a good record and there were many famous people whose lives were touched by it. For example, one of the members of the board of trustees was Major General Clinton Bowen Fisk, who had known both Lincoln and Grant. He founded Fisk University in the south, one of the first schools for African Americans, and had been an official in the Freemen's Bureau.

Bradford Lee Gilbert became a famous, wealthy architect. He had come to America early in the 1870s to work and study. Instead of going to Yale, he went to New York City. He became associated with the McAuley Mission, and he became a Sunday school teacher in the slums. Often he visited his students, and his love and compassion led him up alleys, into tenements with all their poverty, disease, rats, and violence. He saw the people who lived there through the eyes of Jesus. One day the three Jaeger children, Katie, Gertie, and Julius, didn't come to Sunday school. Bradford went and found them. Their father had been drinking hard and he was so drunk he could not stand up. Their mother was upset and the children pleaded with Bradford saying, "Papa wants to go somewhere and stop drinking." Oh! the heartbreak of liquor and the damage it causes to a family. Bradford returned that night, got the father, and brought him to the mission. After much love was poured into that father, Jaeger opened his own rescue mission nine years later. By that time Bradford Gilbert achieved fame and fortune. He still had time for his work in the slums, and he had become a steady, good friend to both Maria and Jerry.

Eight years after Jerry's death, the widow McAuley became Mrs. Bradford Gilbert. Much remained the same. They still continued in the mission, sometimes leading the evening service. A *Christian Herald* reporter wrote:

> The Lord wonderfully prospered Mr. Gilbert in his profession, and when, in 1892 (eight years after Jerry had gone home), he married the widow of his old friend, Jerry McAuley, it was with the determination to so order their united lives that their stewardship should perpetuate the memory of the one they both loved. Since that time Mr. and Mrs. Gilbert have been staunch supporters of God's work in many fields.
>
> Sitting on the vine-covered veranda of his summer home, on the shores of Long Island Sound, Mr. Gilbert talked with the writer lately.
>
> "I was ill a few years ago, and the doctor sent me up here to rest. I didn't realize at the time that God had anything special for me to do here, but somehow it wasn't long before we had some of the Water Street boys up, helping us out with the church meetings. And then the inspiration came to

me: 'Build ye a boat and consecrate it to the uplift of them
who go down to the sea in ships . . . So I said . . .Yes, Lord'
. . . and—there's the boat."

There it lay, rocking gently in the blue waters of City Island's
harbor. Going on board, we found a snowy, graceful launch
which an old Norwegian pilot had consumed the entire winter in building. It was ready for its blessed work of serving as a
"sky-pilot" to the multitude of sailors whose ships "heave-to"
in that vicinity all through the summer months. Truly, it is a
little boat with a big commission. It was interesting to hear
Mr. Gilbert say that "he took more pleasure in designing the
Sky-Pilot than even the Grand Central Station, New York."
    The yacht is built with the wheel-house in the rear, so that
the entire forward deck, capable of seating perhaps twenty-
five, is free for the workers to conduct their meetings. There
are sleeping accommodations for eight people, and the tiny
cabin, with its swing-table, gives promise of many a cosy meal.
Within the cabin a tablet is erected, which bears upon its
surface the keynote of the whole enterprise:
    Just above the little organ are porcelain letters forming
the promise, "Follow me, and I will make you fishers of men."
That same organ has already had a baptism which may well
consecrate it for the work to which it is pledged. Mrs. E. M.
Whittemore, founder of the Door of Hope Mission, held a
fair thirty years ago, and bought that organ with the pro-
ceeds, installing it in the Water Street Mission. Later, it was
used for a while in the Cremorne Mission; then at Hoboken,
and finally in a mountain mission which the Gilberts started
near their former summer home.

Conclusion

Maria had been pulled out of the miry pit. Her heart was changed
and her life was changed, all because Jesus saved her. Today there are
people who have their feet stuck in the miry pit, and the grime clings
to them. Sometimes it shows up on the outside, and it's visibly clear
that they are in the mud. Their lives are in a mess. Other people have
their feet in a miry pit but it doesn't show on the outside. They are
wearing nice clothes and going to work, but their hearts are evil, full
of greed, hate, anger, and bitterness. The list could go on and on.
The pit is a pit. But there is a way to get out of the pit!
    Across North America there are thousands of young women who
will sleep tonight in a place where people love and care for them and

proclaim to them that there is a better way to live, that they don't need to have their lives stuck in a pit of mire and grime. The Savior rescues; He can rescue them from whatever is holding them down in that pit, and He can rescue us, too.

For a lot of young women it is the false security of having a man around that is the mud. They are looking for someone to love, but they're looking in all the wrong places. These women have been mistreated, many times beaten by clubs or fists, and they need the Savior, like Maria did. As they read the Bible they learn that somebody really loves them. The Savior says, "I love you. I love you the way you are; here is hope for your future: you can have a life of love, forgiveness, peace, courage, and joy."

These women need to be encouraged, but things don't get all straightened out overnight! Maria, separated from Jerry for a long time, started reading the Bible, and she started to understand what God was saying to her. And then that glorious spark of salvation that started her transformation took hold in her life. Jerry and Maria needed Christian friends who were like family. There were years that they needed to work on their jobs, to know what love is, to be part of a church, and to become reformed followers of Christ before they could get married. When the two became one in Christ, in a perfect love triangle, their testimonies were so powerful the city has never been the same.

The "McAuley Experiment" is what their little mission was called. People wondered if lives that had sunk so low could really be reformed. Many came to see for themselves: the Whittemores, Fanny Crosby, Helen Campbell, George Kennan, and others. Rescue missions across the North American continent and around the world were started as one convert led another convert, who led another. In fact, there are so many today we can't count them and the cycle keeps going.

Today the New York City Rescue Mission-McAuley Water Street Mission has miracles happen in it every day. It's an amazing place. For example, at Christmastime in 1994 a man came to the mission to make a donation and told the people who work there, "You don't know me. I never had a meal here. I never slept here, but my life was changed here." He explained how he had been using drugs, living in a horrible place, wandering the streets of New York, and his life was a mess. But he saw people gather around the doors of the McAuley Mission at night. One night he saw the group and went over. They went inside the mission for a gospel service, and he sat in the very back in one of the chairs in the corner. He heard about the Savior and accepted the Lord that night in his heart, but he didn't go forward, so the people at the mission didn't know what had happened. But this man found himself in New York City years later, Christmas of 1994. He came into the mission and told them that he had gone to Bible school, had married a Christian woman, is serving the Lord, and is active in his church. People whose lives are touched for just a moment—just a moment—are changed forever. Salvation is the spark that reforms us.

> I waited patiently for the LORD; and he inclined unto me, and heard my cry. He brought me up also out of an horrible pit, out of the miry clay, and set my feet upon a rock, and established my goings. And he hath put a new song in my mouth, even praise unto our God: many shall see it, and fear, and shall trust in the LORD (Psalm 40:1–3 KJV).

Endnotes

1. R. M. Offord, ed., *Jerry McAuley, An Apostle to the Lost* (American Tract Society: New York, 1907), iii.
2. Ibid., 43.
3. William E. Paul, *The Romance of Rescue* (IUGM, 1946), 21.
4. Paul, *Rescue*, 22.
5. Paul, *Rescue*, 23.
6. Arthur Bonner, *Jerry McAuley and His Mission* (Neptune, N.J.: Loizeaux Brothers, 1967), 24.
7. Paul, *Rescue*, 24.
8. Paul, *Rescue*, 25.
9. Bonner, *Mission*, 34.
10. Offord, *Apostle*, 30–31.
11. Paul, *Rescue*, 26.
12. Offord, *Apostle*, 43–45.
13. Paul, *Rescue*, 36–37.
14. Paul, *Rescue*, 38.
15. The following quotes are taken from *Apostle* by Offord, 50–51.

3

Perfect Love Drives Out Fear

Emma Whittemore

God is love. Whoever lives in love lives in God, and God in him. In this way, love is made complete among us so that we will have confidence on the day of judgment, because in this world we are like him. There is no fear in love. But perfect love drives out fear.

—1 John 4:16–18

Introduction

*H*er diamond rings glittered as she picked up a stemmed crystal water glass from the elegant white linen tablecloth at the exclusive tennis club. What was I doing there with one hundred chattering, superficial women dripping with gold? Their charity luncheon would raise little money compared to what they had. All the poor widows give more than these wealthy women. My mind and heart went into the judging mode even deeper. They have so much while others have so little. What a waste of time. I would rather be with "real people," the poor. I was disgusted with the opulence of the women. My mind stopped a second and the Lord whispered in my memory bank, "Judge not, lest you be judged. See them through the eyes of Jesus. Don't judge them any more than you judge the person in the gutter. They need Jesus, too." I started to listen to the woman next to me. She was wealthy, frightened, and lonely.

Wealthy non-Christians are often generous to rescue ministries to the poor. For a few, when they meet the poor face-to-face, they meet the Savior in a powerful way. One couple found the face of Jesus in a most unexpected way.

Emma and Sidney Whittemore kneeled at the little mission's altar with drunks and prostitutes on both sides. They arose up from their knees to do amazing things for God. Emma went into the worst, most dangerous neighborhoods to tell the least, the last, and the lost about Jesus. Today, there are many ministries that were sparked by this compassionate, courageous, wealthy woman. When she left her comfort zone, Jesus whispered to her heart from the Scriptures, "Perfect love casteth out fear" (1 John 4:18 KJV).

⁂

Emma Mott was born into a wealthy family of position. When she married Sydney Whittemore there was even more money, more servants, and life was filled with parties, laughter, ballroom dancing, and all the other pleasures of wealth.

The following story in Emma Whittemore's own words is taken from *Mother Whittemore's Modern Miracles*, edited by F. A. Robinson (Canada: Mission of Bibical Education, 1931).

I was standing before a long mirror in my library awaiting the arrival of the carriage that was to take us to a certain place of entertainment. I stood admiring my beautiful gown. At that time I possessed some very beautiful diamonds which had been given me by my parents. If one wore pearls, it was then the fashion to sprinkle pearl dust over the hair, or if diamonds were worn, diamond dust was the ornamentation. My costume on that particular night was to be a surprise to all my friends. It was supposed to be unusually striking and attractive. Woman-like, I was turning and twisting before a long mirror in my library. I was almost lost in admiration of the beautiful dress and the sparkling diamond dust.

Miss Kelly invited me to go hear Rev. Henry Valley of London, England speak at the Y.M.C.A. . . . My husband had been ignorant of the fact that I was in the building, and I had not the slightest thought that he would be present. . . . By the end of the service our heads were bowed before the Lord as we each endeavored to form firm resolutions to live a different life. It was not until the next Sunday, however, that those resolutions were in reality carried out.

Miss Kelly, who had persuaded me to go to the Valley meeting . . . called again to invite us to go with her to a meeting on Water Street to see Jerry McAuley, the so-called "Living Wonder" of the Fourth Ward. My husband rather reluctantly consented and it was with the distinct understanding that upon no consideration would he take his wife down into that locality more than "this once."

Never can that night be erased from memory. From the time we got off the car at Roosevelt Street, each step seemed to open up some new horror. The night was very dark and the narrow streets were dimly lighted. Curses and . . . quarreling and fighting, on the part of both young and old, were witnessed on all sides. Policemen seemed to be using their clubs upon the slightest provocation, and we saw several poor wretched women dragged off to the Station House. Vulgar and vicious people were crowded into every street along which we walked.

At last the door of the Mission was reached. It had formerly been a little old dance hall, but had been converted into a place of worship. It was very much crowded with sin-bedraggled people and vile smells! We were compelled to go far forward by Jerry's gruff and imperative call, "Come up here, the whole three of you back yonder and sit down." We had not been accustomed to that kind of treatment and at that time knew nothing of the great heart that lay behind Jerry's rough manner.

As we waited for the service to begin, my husband whispered condescending words about the "poor creatures" around us. Certainly they constituted an almost sickening sight. As the meeting progressed, however, God got such possession of him and later on of myself also that we were both held in painful silence as we were convicted of our useless lives. We no longer felt superior to the "poor creatures" around us but actually hung our heads in shame. Then God's Spirit convinced my dear husband that some of these "poor creatures" had something to say to us both if we were willing to listen.

What a gathering it was! After the singing and praying, Jerry read a few verses from the Bible and followed it by a simple but heart-searching explanation of the passage. The strangely moving story of his own conversion was then told in the graphic way that never failed to touch hearts. Immediately thereafter the meeting was thrown open for testimonies. Never before had we witnessed such a sight; no urging was necessary to get the people to take part: three, four, five, were on their feet at the same time, followed in quick succession by others. All were so earnest and so full of gratitude to God for saving them and for keeping them day by day amidst sorest temptations and trials that no one could help being deeply impressed. We knew that these people were truly transformed and possessed the genuine thing and not the veneer that characterized some professed Christians in the social circle that had engrossed our time and thought.

Finally, greatly overcome, my husband rose to his feet and to my astonishment requested prayers from the redeemed men present. He was such a stiff Presbyterian and had been so very conventional and uncompromising, that I could scarcely believe my own eyes. He put his hand to his face to cover his emotion and I saw a tear trickling through his fingers. In spite of my worldly spirit, I thought he had never appeared nobler or braver in my eyes. I could not let him stand alone. Where he would go I would go. I arose and quietly stood by his side. Jerry turned his piercing eyes on us and said in a loud and almost fierce voice, . . . "Did y' mean it, both of y'?" We gave a nod of assent. Yet there were conflicting emotions! We were both strangely affected but I know my pride rebelled at the thought of being prayed for or brought back to God by a thief, even though he was converted. "Then if y' did, come and kneel at this bench." As he spoke, he pointed to an old worm-eaten and none too clean bench. . . . In a few moments there were kneeling about us river-thieves, drunkards, gamblers, and abandoned women of the streets. We had gone there to see Jerry, "the Curiosity of the Fourth Ward," but surely we were successful competitors for that title that night. It had always been our custom to dress for evening dinner, and when we decided to go to see Jerry, we had slipped on our coats, never dreaming we might have to remove them. But the hall was so crowded and had become so hot that we simply had to lay them aside. What curiosities we must have been, attired as we were, in that motley ragged group.

Around us were scantily-clad, unclean, vicious-looking men and women. At last we were kneeling close together in one long line. Jerry stated at one end, "Pray, brother. Yes, y' must. I can pray till the breath leaves my body, but that won't save ye, ye must pray yourselves." Many of the petitions were suggested by Jerry. The majority were "God be merciful to me a sinner."

It never entered my head that Jerry would ask me to pray, and my thoughts were on my husband. What would he say? He used such good English. I had always felt proud of him at social functions when he was called on to speak. I knew that his prayer would be strikingly different to the others.

At last Jerry came to us. He placed a hand on each of our shoulders. I looked up. A tear was zigzagging down the cheek of the man we thought so rough. It fell between us. It was a holy tear shed by a man who yearned to have others accept his Savior. It spoke more loudly to me than any words could have done. He asked Mr. Whittemore to pray. Slowly the words came to his lips, but they were not the words I had anticipated. They were the words the poor blear-eyed drunkard at his side had just stammered out: "God be merciful to me a sinner." In a more tender tone Jerry said, "put in 'for Jesus sake'" I have always said since that those three words are God's cover of love, hiding away all our sins.

Suddenly the Spirit began witnessing with ours that we were acceptable in His sight once more through the blood-cleansing process and power of Jesus. Wanderers we had been, but the seeking Shepherd had found us! We arose with a holy determination, born of God Himself, to hence-forth live for His glory and praise. From that night I date the giving up of a worldly life. . . .

And Jesus, when he came out, saw much people, and was moved with compassion towards them, because they were as sheep not having a Shepherd: and he began to teach them many things (Mark 6:34).

As the days grew into weeks, such an intensity for souls was experienced that it seemed almost impossible for us to keep away from the place that we were to have visited "only once." Though we were ever perfectly conscious that the folly and disobedience to our God had been all blotted out and forgiven, the memory of those wasted years could not be erased. More than once that memory was used to keep us in our right places, and through the promptings of the Holy Spirit, it encouraged absolute surrender to Him to whom we had formerly been so disloyal (pp. 18–24).

One evening I spent some time alone with God earnestly inquiring of Him, "as He would be inquired of," what was to be done with my own wonderful healing so graciously given. Most earnestly did I desire to know what would be most to His glory. Suddenly the girls on the street came to my mind so forcibly that it was not difficult to almost imagine I could hear the tramp of numberless feet going straight to damnation. Something innate, however, caused a shrinking from it all, for up to this time I had ever felt such a loathing for anything bordering upon impurity that I never could tolerate a wicked woman. Even when in the Mission, where they would sometimes come, I always gave plenty of opportunity to the other workers to labor amongst them rather than get into close contact with them myself. Thus it appeared almost impossible and even repellent to think of yielding to the suggestion which had entered my mind. Even though grateful for all I had received, I could not for an instant refrain from saying: "Surely, Lord, it cannot be for me to mingle with those I have so decidedly scorned and despised? Oh, anything but that! Much as I love Thee and for all that Thou hast bestowed on me, surely that cannot be my work."

After thus almost foolishly informing Him of that of which He was perfectly aware, a deep hush of shame settled upon my heart, and in the stillness which followed, He caused me to realize that there was in my heart a serious lack of love for such a class, and in great gentleness He gave me distinctly to understand that though He does not hold one responsible for traits not naturally possessed, He does hold one responsible for not accepting His unchangeable love. The Holy Spirit then brought to my remembrance "With God all things are possible," and clearly showed me that if I was disobedient to this call, I should miss large opportunity of service and blessing.

With this, there came such a divine revelation of what might be expected through complying, and how every necessary equipment would be furnished, that finally all opposition became dissolved in that great Love. Arising from my knees with a heart full of adoration and praise, I prayerfully assented to His wishes, surprised only that He should deign to take one so unworthy to carry out His will in this special line of service.

We started out in the late afternoon with a holy desire created by God, to carry some ray of light to those who in the darkness of sin were stumbling along, ignorant of the fact of His pardoning and compassionate love.

The horrors we witnessed nearly overpowered us. Often after such nights of tramping the streets, have I dropped upon my knees as I reached home and in tears cried out, "Oh! Lord, I cannot, I cannot see these fearful sights again! It simply breaks my heart." Then I could almost hear the pleading, compassionate voice of Jesus whispering: "Be still and know that I am God" and in that sacred stillness, when every thought was held in divine subjection, comforting promises for the work came quick and fast. An increase of His love was the outcome, and before arising I could feel the divine force impelling me to go steadfastly onward as He might lead.

Rebuffs? Yes, we encountered many of them, but as we became acquainted with God and His methods, they ceased to have much weight. Oh worker, turn a deaf ear to the insults! Be blind to the scornful look! Penetrate behind them all into the sinners' hearts! They may be desperately vile but extend to them unceasingly the message of God, even if it should be seemingly rejected. If communicated continually in God-given love, those poor bruised victims will perceive the Christ-like persistency and they will find the way of escape from their sinful paths.

I was standing one day in the parlor of a house that it would not be profitable to describe, but where everything that money could purchase was provided to attract the eye and distract one's thoughts from that which was right. A young girl of sixteen was in the ungodly group that frequented the place. Pretty in face and elegantly though scantily dressed, and deeply dyed in sin she stood, apparently enjoying herself, smoking a highly-flavored cigarette.

Upon approaching her and uttering a few kind words, she laughed rudely and tossed her little head as she deliberately puffed a mouthful of smoke into my face. This was her only reply. For a moment I was almost suffocated. She laughed loudly at the effect the smoke had on me. Praying for guidance, a conversation commenced. Seemingly it merely amused her and was an invitation to her to become bolder and more insolent. Every few seconds she laughingly blew more smoke into my face, and replied saucily to whatever was said. When she came to the end of her cigarette and was about lighting another, it seemed as if God breathed very gently into my heart the words, "Now!" and "Love!" Quickly I felt impelled to place my arm around her and said: "Child, you have treated me most rudely and you know it. You've laughed, sneered, and ridiculed almost everything I have attempted to say, but tell me dear, tell me truly (pointing to her heart), is there any laughter down there?"

An amazing transformation took place. With a half smothered sob, she glanced nervously around to see if she were observed by the Madam of that awful place, who sat but a short distance away. Seeing that the Madam's attention was elsewhere, she answered in a sort of smothered whisper: "Oh, no ma'am. God knows there is no laughter nor happiness there! How could there be?" "You poor child," I replied, "tell me the honest truth. Would you do differently if you had a chance?" An almost incredulous and surprised look akin to fear was upon her face as she quickly answered, "Indeed I would, but I can't, I can't." She shook her head as she said despondently, "I wouldn't be let."

"Well, my dear, you just shall have a chance," was all I could say, as I drew her close to my side. Still fearful of being discovered in serious conversation, she nevertheless expressed such gratitude that I discovered God had made it possible to reach the heart that had at first seemed so callous and so fast closed to everything good. Jesus became very real, and the difficulties that seemed insurmountable to us were not to Him. He had gained an entrance to her heart and ere many days the poor child was liberated from all the horrors that were attached to the fearful life she had been leading (pp. 41–44).

Having two empty beds at the Door of Hope, most earnestly was the Lord requested that they might be occupied by those with whom He desired us to labor. A short time afterwards, a Bible reader brought us a little Jewish girl about fifteen years of age. Her story was most pitiful. She had been betrayed and then cruelly deserted and would have been left utterly friendless, unless willing to relinquish her baby. After a brief conversation I informed her that we had not thought of taking children. Before I could explain any further, big tears flowed down her face as she said: "Oh, I'd rather walk the streets and starve with my baby in my arms than to have a place to stay and give him up. Every place I've been refuses to take me because I have a baby but I just won't give him up. I love him too much to let him go."

I concluded it was no time for talking, so simply replied: "Well, dear, let us kneel together and ask what the Lord wants us to do." With my arm around the trembling shoulders I could somehow better appreciate the depths of the motherly love that was in her heart even though she was only a child herself. Feeling somehow impressed that there was the chord that might vibrate with praises to His glory from her life, I offered fervent prayer in her behalf and before arising from our knees, the matter was settled. I pressed a kiss on her cheek as I said: "Hannah, dear child, I'll take you both. You may bring your baby." Throwing her arms around my neck and weeping with joy, the child-mother explained, "Oh, then I can, I can have my baby, my own dear little baby!"

Going out of the room, I sought the matron and informed her of my decision. She naturally expressed some surprise, as we both could not but agree that the Home at that early stage of the work was scarcely a suitable place for an infant. Seeing that I believed it to be God's will, she answered: "Well, then, it is of no use for me to say anything more." She added in an impressively serious tone, "but I hope you realize that a baby means we must get more milk and you know how hard it is to get supplies now." I could scarcely regard the matter as so threateningly serious so I jokingly responded: "That is a tremendous problem! Still, my dear, if another mouth is really sent here to be filled, our God is capable of sending the baby's milk or any other thing that is necessary." Thus the matter was settled (pp. 93–94).

One evening in the 32nd Street Mission, Mrs. McAuley leaned over and whispered: "A Madam of one of those gilded dens near here has sent today for someone to take a very sick girl away and do something for her. Do you know where she could be put? Could she go to the Door of Hope?" I shook my head, answering quietly, "I don't know of any place for

her; it would never do to let such a girl come to the Door of
Hope: in her condition she would probably die." I had learned
how superstitious the girls are and I felt it might prejudice
others whom we wished to reach. We could not afford to run
such a risk.

As these objections flashed through my mind, just as suddenly did it occur to me, that I had not asked the Lord what
He desired. Silently a request was lifted from my heart and as
silently came the gentle reminder: "Inasmuch as ye did it unto
one of . . ." Before the verse was finished I eagerly leaned forward and grasping Mrs. McAuley by the hand, said, "I'll take
her myself." With a look of real relief, she said: "God bless
you. Suppose we go to see her at once." Slipping quietly out of
the meeting, we hastened to the place of evil a few blocks off
and found the girl dying of tuberculosis. Upon investigation,
we discovered she had been sorely neglected and had been
subsisting for over six weeks on beer, her stomach resisting all
food. She was a pitiful sight and our hearts were sickened and
sad. It was easy to see that she had "spent all." Once she had
been the most attractive girl at many a New York ball. People
would actually wait to see her leave the building and enter the
carriage. It was worth waiting to be able to gaze upon her beauty
and upon her elegant garments.

At first she positively refused to leave the wretched place
in which we found her. She impatiently informed us that she
knew all about such homes, they were "like prisons." She
was "too sick to be bothered." "What did it matter now!"
She did "not want to go anywhere." Seeing that attempted
persuasion was only exciting her, I knelt by the bedside saying: "No matter, dear, we did not mean to vex you. I'll just
have prayer before going." Such a wave of divine tenderness
swept over me that I could hardly articulate what I wished to
be conveyed to her heart. Before I arose from my knees, she
stretched forth her wasted white hands and nervously clasping mine, said with tears in her eyes: "I'll go! I'll go to the
Door of Hope. I will!"

She was brought up the next day on pillows in a carriage.
She had scarcely been placed upon the comfortable bed when
she began to wildly cry, "Beer, beer; I must have beer!" The
physician, who accompanied her, beckoned me aside and ar-
gued that though as a rule he disapproved of prescribing beer,
yet in this case he could see no alternative. He felt compelled
to order its use.

After a moment's thought, I positively refused to furnish it, not only because opposed to any sort of liquor, but because of other girls who had arrived that very day. I considered them as precious in God's sight and needing salvation fully as much as poor Vangie herself. If these girls knew that beer was in the house, the temptation might be too strong for them to resist.

Others who were present pleaded with me to meet the doctor's wishes, but at last seeing how determined I was, the doctor withdrew, saying somewhat gravely: "Then you must take the consequences, and it is a very serious one in my estimation."

A few minutes later the doorbell rang and in came Mrs. Kinney, a true woman of God. Noticing my evident distress and upon being quickly informed of the cause, she pressed my hand sympathetically. That look and that touch were like an inspiration. Leading her quietly into the reception room, I said: "Oh, Mrs. Kinney, can't you unite your faith with mine and just trust God to deliver that poor sick girl upstairs from this cursed appetite?" Calmly and confidently came the answer, "Certainly dear. Yes, we shall ask Him and He will do it." Such a peace entered my heart that we knelt with great assurance and claimed the victory. A worker stood at the door as we arose from our knees and we were informed that the girl had fallen asleep. It proved something more than a restful slumber, for, upon awakening, she stated that all longing for opium and beer had disappeared.

This was still more forcibly impressed upon us the next day when two of her former companions called and managed to smuggle two bottles of liquor under their capes into her room. One of them pushed a bottle along the quilt but Vangie shook her head. They tried to induce her to accept it but with great firmness in her weak tones she waved her hand emphatically, saying: "Take it away. Take it away. I have no need for that any more. I am through with it forever." Then more tenderly added, "Not now Annie: I've lived miserably but I'm going to die happy."

The following day, realizing what God had accomplished by His Holy Spirit, it was not difficult to convince her that He was capable of blotting out her sins. She had recalled all that miserable wretched past and as she did so many a shudder quivered through her frame. At last the light dawned and she gladly accepted her Savior. Very shortly afterwards, through the witnessing of God's Spirit, she began to rejoice at being set free from the thraldom, which, for so long a time had held her. From that hour she thought no more of opium, morphine, or alcohol.

Many friends visited that sick room, and their faith in God was greatly strengthened thereby. Though Vangie appreciated their sympathetic and loving attention and also the many gifts they brought, she would repeatedly say, as her face lighted up with intelligent joy: "Oh, this is not just done for me half as much, Mother Whittemore, as it is because they have the love of God and do it for His sake. Isn't He good?"

On Thanksgiving morning, a marked change was observed and one could plainly see that her life was drawing to a close. Contrary to my usual custom in praying daily that all-sufficient grace be supplied to meet the day's need, I was led, after a brief talk and reading of Scripture, to ask most definitely as I knelt by her side, that an abundant entrance might be granted when the summons came and that all through the intervening hours a foretaste of Heaven should be experienced.

While thus engaged, her father who had held her hand in his own for hours, became so convulsed with grief that I offered up a brief petition in his behalf. Fearing he would disturb her, I arose and taking him by the hand led him into the hall. I could not but notice how he trembled and during a few words of earnest conversation he looked at me with a silent but perceptible yearning. Great tears silently trickled down his cheeks as I said: "Mr. B., just think, this is Thanksgiving day and if ever a father had great cause to return thanks to God, you surely have. See what He has actually accomplished for your child! Why not thank Him in earnest by giving Him your heart? He has waited so long and He loves you."

He listened attentively to every word and then firmly clasping both of my hands, he said with much emotion: "I will, God helping me. Yes, I take Him for my God." His darling child was immediately informed of the good news and her very soul seemed overflowing with glory as she endeavored to express her gratitude. From that time on she did not want him to leave her for a moment.

The next few hours she occupied in giving various commissions and in leaving loving messages for former friends. Especially did she thank the one who had attended her more constantly than others of us were privileged to do. I remained by her bedside, for I knew the home-going would not be long delayed. After resting a little, she lifted her arm and lovingly placed it around my neck. In a most caressing way she patted my cheek, saying: "Oh, Mother Whittemore, may our Lord God bless you!" I promptly replied, "Yes, He has blessed me dear, and through you; I thank Him for ever letting you come here."

The answer was a look of glad and grateful surprise which increased as I went on to more fully explain. It spoke louder than words. In a moment or two she began to quietly pray in a most touching manner for one of her former comrades in sin. The words came slowly and brokenly for her strength was almost gone. It was the last deep yearning for another wayward soul. I then asked her if she had any message for the girls with whom she formerly associated.

The very brightness of heaven seemed to beautify her as she replied: "Oh, yes; tell Milly to give herself to Christ." Though no clue to this poor girl for whom she was so burdened could ever be discovered, who can tell but in answer to prayer this book may some day fall into her hands and she will be made immediately to know who was personally meant by our dear Vangie.

So did our Lord lead her lovingly on to the very Borderland. When about crossing over, with the Glory-light upon her dying face, she lifted up both her hands, saying with tender emphasis: "I am going, I am going." She then asked us to sing "Just As I Am" and as the last words "Here for a season, then above, O Lamb of God, I come" were being sung, she became absent from the body and present with the Lord (pp. 72–78).

> Just as I am, without one plea
> But that Thy blood was shed for me.
> And that thou bidd'st me come to Thee,
> Oh, Lamb of God, I come, I come.
> —Charlotte Elliot

Conclusion

Desperate times demand divine deliverance. While listening to women staff members at a shelter, I asked, "What kind of materials do you need?" A young black woman cried out, "We need more material on deliverance." Sidney and Emma Whittemore were delivered from selfishness, Vangie from alcohol and drugs. Whatever the "mud" is, the helping hand of God miraculously pulls us out if we let him do it! "Reach down your hand from on high; deliver me and rescue me from the mighty waters" (Ps. 144:7). Biblical truth is the greatest material on the subject and a changed life is the testimony.

Mother Whittemore was professional. She called in a physician and used medical advice and help when needed. Her home was orderly, with clean beds, good food, and discipline. She and her coworkers used lots of TLC—Tender Loving Care—as they stayed by Vangie's side.

The parallels between the Nasmiths and Mother Whittemore and our current wave of Christian women and family shelters, started in the 1960s to 70s, are amazing. They started with compassion and love for women with need and soon developed into specialized programs. Each is independent with local boards so they can meet the particular changing needs of the community where they are part of faith ministries.

The untold story is that rescue missions and other Christian ministries house more homeless women, children, and men than any other group. Some of the current programs include: emergency shelters, shelters for abused women, long-term rehabilitation, special programs for alcohol and drug treatment, educational programs—high school completion (GED), individualized computer learning centers, ongoing remedial reading programs, job skills and life skills programs—homes for unwed mothers, crisis pregnancy centers, transitional housing, specific after-care follow-up programs, family ministries, neighborhood visitation programs, extended housing, family counseling and guidance services, furniture, food, clothing, and medical and dental care. Because so many of the mentally ill are homeless, we have many in our programs. Growing programs are: special services for the mentally ill, client-payee programs, separate residential programs, day care drop-in centers, special ministries to senior citizens, senior residences, nursing homes, regular visitation of shut-ins. Not all ministries have been listed. They all, however, have Bible studies, chapel, and so on, and therefore can get to the root of the problems: forgiveness, motivation, hope, peace, and love. Many of the staff are women who have been rescued themselves; some have earned college degrees.

Mother Whittemore, with her husband, was cofounder of the International Union of Gospel Missions (IUGM), the association of rescue missions. In 1913 her husband was the first president for a short time, and at the first annual meeting she was unanimously elected the IUGM's second president and served for four years, during which she built the solid foundation upon which rests her purpose, as stated in the 1915 annual report, to

> Further the interests and increase the effectiveness of Gospel Missions . . . to acquaint the Christian public with the growth and importance of this organization. It is a well established fact that unity means strength, and rescue work has developed to such an extent it seemed imperative for the rescue missions to band together in such a way as to let the world know they are doing something worthwhile for the Master.

Years later, "The Bible is still our rule," as it was with Nasmith; lives are being changed, the hungry are fed, the homeless are sheltered, the jobless find jobs, the hopeless find hope, the violent find victory. Those who are the problem become the solution. Maria and Emma led us into the 1900s with love, compassion, commitment, and courage, and it is with great joy we look forward to the year 2000.

As the need has increased, God has been faithful. In the last seven years rescue ministries affiliated with the IUGM have seen their budgets increase from 50 million dollars to 350 million dollars, most given by loving, compassionate women. Jesus started it all with the Sermon on the Mount, and others followed. David and Frances Nasmith laid the foundation of city missions in the early 1800s, Maria and Jerry McAuley and Sidney and Emma Whittemore led the way in the late 1800s, and today, in the late 1900s, there are thousands of women, many of color, who are leading the way to the 2000s with courage, commitment, compassion, and love!

God is love. Mother Whittemore lived in love, lived in God, and God lived in Mother Whittemore. In this way love was made complete in Mother Whittemore so that she would have confidence on the Day of Judgment, because in this world she was like him. She had no fear in love because perfect love drives out fear (a definition of Mother Whittemore in the context of the Scripture, 1 John 4:16–18). Like Maria McAuley, Emma Whittemore didn't become living love overnight.

Emma Whittemore went to the mission five nights a week and saw the love and compassion of Jerry and Maria McAuley (pp. 32, 61–63). She learned how to give her testimony and became a mission worker. Maria taught Emma how to work with girls and women and took Mother Whittemore to her old hang outs. This led to the founding of the first Door of Hope, which was dedicated in 1890 by

A. B. Simpson. Mrs. McAuley and other mission people were there. At the time of Mother Whittemore's death there were ninety-seven Door of Hopes around the world.[1] The number grew to about 250. Although not all bore the name of Door of Hope many became gospel rescue missions. She gave her first Door of Hope and Tappan Home to the Salvation Army and became an honorary staff captain (pp. 112, 154).

Mother Whittemore helped start missions, found superintendents for them, and became the superintendent of the Gospel Mission with the assistance of her husband (pp. 97–105, 248–52).

Moved by the needs of children, Emma founded a kindergarten in a violent neighborhood where bullets sometimes came through the windows. She wrote a book, *Delia the Bluebird of Mulberry Bend*, the story of a violent young woman of the "underworld." Delia reached over one hundred of her friends for Christ. The book became a best-seller printed in twelve languages.[2]

Emma became internationally known as she was invited to speak all over the world. God used her as she inspired others to form independent gospel rescue ministries in their own cities. Like Nasmith, Emma believed in local control.

Endnotes

1. Daniel G. Reid, ed., *Dictionary of Christianity in America* (Downers Grove, Ill.: InterVarsity Press, 1990), 1254.
2. Emma M. Whittemore, *Delia, The Bluebird of Mulberry Bend* (Old Tappan, N.J.: Fleming H. Revell, 1893–1914), 3.

Bibliography

Roger Greenway, *Discipling the City* (Baker Book House: Grand Rapids, 1992).

Norris Magnuson, *Salvation in the Slums* (Grand Rapids: Baker, 1977).

Marvin Olasky, *The Tragedy of American Compassion* (Washington, D.C.: Regnery Publishing, 1995).

William E. Paul, *The Romance of Rescue*, 2d ed. (Minneapolis: Osterhus, 1959).

Ruth A. Tucker, *Guardians of the Great Commission* (Grand Rapids: Zondervan, 1988).

Let Your Light Shine

Clemme Ellis White

No Creed but Christ, No Law but Love!

Introduction

$\mathcal{T}$he closing call at the second Triennial Conference of the City Mission World Association in Washington, D.C., which brought together rescue mission leaders from over thirty countries around the world, was given by Dr. Paul Toaspern, who had been secretary of the city missions in East Germany during the Communist era.

In calling the church to remember the city and the need for compassion, love, and commitment, he recited a poem he had seen on the wall of St. Paul's House, a mission outreach in Hell's Kitchen, New York City.

I said, "Let me walk in the fields."
God said, "Nay, walk in the town."
I said, "There are no flowers there."
He said, "No flowers, but a crown."
I said: "But the skies are black, nothing but noise and din."
And He wept—as He sent me back.
"There is more," He said, "There is sin."
I said, "But the air is sick and flocks are veiling the sun."
He answered, "Yet souls are sick,
and souls in the dark are undone."
I answered, "I shall miss the light,
and friends will miss me, they say."
He answered, "Choose tonight, if I'm to miss you or they."
I pleaded for time to be given . . .
He said, "Is it too hard to decide?
It will not seem hard in Heaven,
who have followed the steps of your guide;
I cast one look at the fields, then set my face at the town.
He said, "My child, do you yield?
Will you leave the flowers for the crown?"
Then into His hand went mine, and into my heart came He.
And I walked in a light divine—the part I had feared to see.

That call, badly needed today, was written in the early part of the twentieth century by Clemme Ellis White, a missionary to the city of New York, an ordained minister at a time when women were not considered proper ministers. She was a farm girl whose heart for the city went far beyond New York. She became a national leader in urban ministry as one of the founders of the International Union of Gospel Missions, its secretary, an editor, and the oracle for the rescue mission movement. She served as editor of *Our Missions*, as well

as a member of the mostly male IUGM executive committee from
1919 to 1949. She was named Honorary Secretary and Historian in
1949 and served until her death in 1960 at age eighty-seven.

✿❧❀❦❀

As the poem suggests, Clemme Ellis was a country girl. Born in
1873, she was raised in a devout Christian farm home, and after gradu-
ating from Patty Normal School at age fifteen, she became a district
school teacher. Clemme remembers her childhood:

> I was born and reared in the pretty little village of
> Clintondale in upstate New York. My father was a farmer.
> He and my mother worked hard to maintain for myself and
> my two brothers a comfortable home and to give us educa-
> tional advantages. My parents cared where we went and with
> whom. Even had I wished to stray from the "straight and
> narrow" their supervision would have made it difficult.[1]

Clemme grew up in Sunday school and church, and early learned
to know herself to be a sinner and found in Jesus Christ a personal
Savior. Her mother, living to a few months of "rounding out a century of life," was a great influence on Clemme's entire life. "It was at
her knees," Clemme would recall, "that I learned to pray and from
her lips. I often listened as she read the old gospel stories from the
Book."
Clemme as a girl felt a call to preach but pushed it aside knowing
that to most it was men's work.

> When I was but a girl I felt the call to preach. . . . And yet
> I argued with myself, trying to prove that it was not my call-
> ing. I felt I could not enter into a field where women were
> comparatively unknown.[2]

So to be a teacher or maybe a medical doctor seemed more rea-
sonable goals. In 1890, at age seventeen, Clemme went to New York
City to teach and study for a medical career.

> I planned a medical career, . . . planning to make teaching
> a means to my end. But God . . . showed me the city's great
> need and called me to surrender my will to His, that under
> His direction I might find in rescue mission circles an avenue
> of usefulness.[3]

Shortly after arriving in New York Clemme accepted an invitation that changed the direction of her life and made an imprint on thousands of broken men, women, and children in the city of New York and the rescue mission movement. It brought back that call on her life to minister but in an environment she did not understand and to people that were scary to her. In Clemme's words:

> After getting settled in New York City and entering my work there as a teacher, I was invited to address a mission service. My old friend who made this engagement escorted me one evening to the heart of Chinatown to the Old Rescue Society's Mission in Doyers Street. What a motley crowd of men, dirty and drunk! There was a smaller group of such women as I had not known existed. This was my introduction to rescue missions. As I sat on the platform I was a scared country girl who felt that if she could escape alive she would never again project herself into such company. But then as they sang an old gospel song there came to my heart the conviction that these folk needed what I had to make them new in Jesus Christ. I could hardly wait until this song was finished to grasp the privilege of telling the "Story of Love." From that day until this I have loved the rescue mission and found in it my field of endeavor.[4]

Clemme became friends with a young minister and his wife who superintended the Door of Hope Mission under the direction of Sidney and Emma Whittemore. Once each week Clemme spoke the evening message. She became a weekly dinner guest at the Whittemores and was asked to take permanent charge of the mission. Clemme states that "after much spiritual conflict I gave up my plan for a medical career and assumed charge of the West Side Gospel Mission."

The mission was in the Theater District with Hell's Kitchen to the west and the Tenderloin District to the south. Each night Clemme went on the street to conduct an open-air service before the evening gospel service in the mission. A "little wisp of a girl," Clemme would use a bull horn to be heard. It must have been quite a picture to see this quiet country girl, the refined school teacher by day and evangelist by night, doing what a few years before she would have never thought she would be doing.

Opposition developed. The grocer's wife, who resented Clemme in the proximity of their grocery store, ran a counterattraction. With the help of other store clerks using tin pans, the clerks attempted to disrupt the meeting. Instead, this just brought out a larger crowd.

Clemme never forgot the night, "As my voice carried well and I could not ask anyone else to attempt speaking in that noise, I did my best to get the gospel over to the crowd."[5]

Instead of a disaster, God used the din—the noise and the crowd—and the slip of a girl preaching the Gospel to attract the attention of Harry C. White. Harry, a salesman who had strayed from God, followed Clemme back to the mission, made a commitment to Christ, and became a helper at the mission. And then in 1904, they became helpmates for life, as Clemme Ellis became Clemme Ellis White. Harry became the assistant superintendent of the mission.

Clemme continued to teach days at Public School 113 and operate the mission at night and weekends for a number of years.

> This did not interfere with my attendance at the meetings. I did not have a great deal of time to spare as the open air meetings began at seven o'clock in the evening, and at the closing at eight we go into the mission, and hold another meeting until ten. I loved the work, though, and I was never tired.
>
> Finally I decided to give up my teaching . . . and devote all my time to the other work. I shall always be glad of my teaching experience, though. I feel that having been self-supporting was a great asset to me in my work. I feel somehow, that the men and women with whom I work have greater respect for me because I have shown I can earn my own living.[6]

That respect went beyond those to whom she ministered, for other mission workers were impressed with what Clemme was accomplishing. Besides helping other missions, she and Harry opened the Community Gospel Mission in 1910, working with neighborhood poor families. And in 1913, with her mentors, Sidney and Emma Whittemore, Clemme helped found the International Union of Gospel Missions, for she had a strong belief that rescue missions were needed throughout the world.

Clemme became an outstanding leader. She was elected secretary in 1919 and served as the only woman member of the executive committee for thirty years. She traveled through the cities of the United States and Canada visiting missions, encouraging workers, preaching the Gospel, and spreading the word of what was happening in the rescue missions.

A prolific writer, Clemme wrote the definition of rescue missions with her tract, "The Rescue Mission," which has been used for over seventy years and is still defining rescue missions.

The Rescue Mission
by Rev. Clemme Ellis White

What Is a Rescue Mission?

A Rescue Mission is a soul saving place; a place where human wreckage is salvaged through the making over of lives by the Gospel's power. It is an oasis in a desert of despair; a haven of hope for the homeless and heavy-hearted; the salvage department of the church; the church at work downtown every night of the year. The rescue mission is truly an arm of the church working in the dark places of our big cities, and usually in the slum districts.

By the grace of God, it is able not only to put a new suit on a man, but much more important, to put a new man in the suit.

The mission is a relief society, an employment bureau, a reading and rest room, a restaurant, the poor man's hotel, a place to be fumigated in and where one may get a bath. The mission is a place devoted to the reconditioning, the rehabilitating of human derelicts who have been wrecked by the storms of life. The mission is a spiritual awakener, a crime preventer; it is a soul saving and a life saving institution. Our missions keep the spiritual supreme; in a mission under the power of the Gospel, which is daily proclaimed, men are changed from liabilities to assets, from loafers to laborers. The mission does not pauperize men, instead it helps men to help themselves.

Who Founded It?

Jesus Christ, the first mission man, the founder of the rescue mission, perpetually identified Himself with mission work and continuously interested Himself in that group which every rescue mission seeks to reach. Hear Him as He reads, "The Spirit of the Lord is upon me, because he hath anointed me to preach the gospel to the poor; he hath sent me to heal the brokenhearted, to preach deliverance to the captives and recovering of sight to the blind, to set at liberty them that are bruised" (Luke 4:18 KJV).

Hear Him again as He outlines the program of the rescue mission, "I was an hungred and ye gave me meat; I was thirsty, and ye gave me drink: I was a stranger, and ye took me in: Naked and ye clothed me: I was sick and ye visited me; I was in prison and ye came unto me" (Matt. 25:35–36 KJV).

Nothing was nearer to the heart of our Lord than real
mission work and nothing is more scriptural than the work
of the real rescue mission. [Edited]

As editor of *Our Mission*, the quarterly publication of the International Union of Gospel Missions, she wrote the story of rescue and
its movement across the continent, sharing the testimonies of Billy
Sunday and Mel Trotter, rescue mission converts who became great
evangelists. Mission leaders have looked to her writing to study and
understand the movement.

Aware that denominational and doctrinal differences can destroy
cooperative ministry, Clemme used her position and prestige to promote unity. Her theme was No Creed but Christ, No Law but Love,
and she championed it in her speeches and articles. She knew that
people must keep their eyes on a common goal and that a vision of
that goal must be continually reinforced.

Dr. W. E. Paul, former IUGM president, in his book, *Romance of
Rescue*, states:

> [Her] office became the center of information regarding
> vacancies, available workers, Mission fields as well as Mis-
> sion problems. Mrs. White has served the union over a longer
> period of time than any other person, and her tact and wis-
> dom during the early period following the organization, prob-
> ably saved the union for Missions of America.[7]

Clemme promoted the idea of a national headquarters facility to
hold the records of this movement of God that had swept the country in the early twentieth century (over ninety rescue missions were
started in a ten-year period).[8] She willed the funds upon her death
for the first national headquarters building, which was named for
her and was located in Winona Lake, Indiana.[9] The IUGM has since
moved to Kansas City, Missouri. The present-day library and re-
source center, where many of Clemme's works are preserved, are a
fulfillment of Clemme's vision.

The issue of women preaching the Gospel is not a new argument.
In most churches at the turn of the century it was frowned upon, as it
still is in many churches. It has always been more acceptable for a
woman to do parish or missionary work but not acceptable for a
woman to be ordained. When Clemme Ellis White was ordained in
1920 during an IUGM meeting, the *New York Evening Telegraph*'s
headlines stated: "Women Access to Ministry Makes New Era in
History: Ordination of Mrs. May Lindsey Haight and Mrs. Clemme

White vindication of Excommunication in 1638 of Anne Hutchinson for Preaching the Gospel."

Clemme was not afraid to speak her views about women in the ministry. At her ordination, she stated:

> Surely there must have been many other women like me, who perhaps did not possess the courage that I did. They are splendid women with great ability. They have been deviated from a path into which they could have accomplished much good and have turned their energies into business channels. The church has been the loser. In pursuing the policy which it [the church] has toward women in the ministerial field, it has made a terrible mistake, which time alone can right.[10]

Clemme Ellis White accomplished "much good," and even though she became a national leader in rescue missions, her heart was always on Broadway at the West Side Mission. With Harry at her side until his death in 1936, and then until her retirement in 1949, she kept telling the story of love, and her joy was in those who responded, for she became part of their lives. The *Evening Telegraph* reporter interviewing Clemme on her ordination made note of a telephone call "from a young woman who had been converted in the mission and who had made Mrs. White the personal confidante of her troubles. Now she was happily married and anxious that Mrs. White come to the birthday party of one of her children." As Clemme hung up the phone she told the reporter, "That is one of the compensations of my work." The heart of rescue is the heart of the people of rescue.

New York City was not just the birthplace of the American rescue mission movement, but it was where women excelled in ministry to the poor: Emma Whittemore, Maria McAuley, Clemme Ellis White, and Sarah Wray from the Eighth Avenue Mission, the women of the Missionary Workers, Evangeline Booth and the Salvation Army. Their compassion, love, and courage were the banner unfurled of the movement in New York City.

"Bring the right way to the white way," was Clemme's battle cry, as she was that "light shining in a dark place" (2 Pet. 1:19). But her vision and compassion extended beyond the city to a world in need of rescue. In every edition of *Our Mission* magazine, she stated,

> Somewhere, some way, sometime, each day, I'll turn aside and pray that God will bless all rescue missions and their converts and each member of the IUGM.

New York City, the church of Jesus Christ, and the rescue mission movement were blessed that this shy country girl who wanted to walk in the fields chose the city instead, and, as she wrote:

> I cast one look at the fields, then set my face at the town,
> He said, "My child, do you yield,
> will you leave the flowers for the crown?"[11]
> Then into His hand went mine, and into my heart came He.
> And I walked in a light divine—the part I had feared to see.

Quotes

The Rescue Mission reached those most desperately in need of the message and ministry of the Gospel. With her legitimate field of action among the lost, the last and the least, she obeys the Gospel command.

The homeless are sheltered and fed, in many missions opportunity is afforded those who do not ask charity but a chance to earn their daily bread, the privilege of being self supporting. Laborers and white collared men, many of whom find it a new experience to be out of a job, too proud to beg and too honest to steal but desperate because of conditions for which they are not responsible, are assisted by our Missions through the aid and support of Christian friends.

The Rescue Mission owes the success of its work to the fact that it has kept the spiritual supreme; that she faithfully proclaims the Gospel message.

When inner conditions are changed and made right, exterior conditions soon conform and difficulties are surmounted or dissolved.

Endnotes

The following material can be found in the William Wooley Library at the International Union of Gospel Missions, Kansas City, Missouri.

1. Clemme Ellis White, "From the Country-side to the Great White Way."
2. The *New York Evening Telegraph*, October 3, 1920.
3. White, "Great White Way."

4. Ibid.
5. Ibid.
6. White, quoted in the *Evening Telegraph*.
7. William E. Paul, *Romance of Rescue* (Minneapolis: Osterhus, 1959).
8. Graden J. Grobe, *History of the IUGM*, 1960.
9. *Our Missions* (Kansas Ciry: IUGM), July 1961.
10. White, quoted in the *Evening Telegraph*.
11. White, "Great White Way."

Additional Reading

Our Missions (Kansas City: IUGM), July 1938, 1939, 1940, 1941; April 1949.

5

Home Missionary

Fanny J. Crosby

*It is the most wonderful work in the world and it gives such an
opportunity for love. That is all people want—love.*
                                                        —*Fanny Crosby*

Introduction

We had just put in a dorm for men who have nowhere to go after they leave the hospital and still have special needs. One of the men came in. I had never seen anyone before who did not have a body from the chest down. He was in a homemade wooden cart with two large bicycle wheels he pushed with his hands. He was young, good-looking, tan, had a great beard, and his shoulders and arms swelled with muscles. He was a Viet Nam veteran, and he lived at the mission. He lived with us for months before I asked, "There is so little of your body. How can you live like that?"

His face lighted up as he picked up his huge, worn, brown leather Bible, exclaiming, "All I need is right here!" He continued passionately, "My purpose in life, my call is to reach these men here at the mission for Jesus."

The people some would call weak and handicapped have been some of our most able and productive workers in rescue.

> For ye see your calling, brethren, how that not many wise men after the flesh, not many mighty, not many noble, are called: but God hath chosen the foolish things of the world to confound the wise; and God hath chosen the weak things of the world to confound the things which are mighty (1 Corinthians 1:26–27 KJV).

It was an important night in the life of Mrs. Alexander Van Alsyne, Fanny Crosby. It was the night that she made a new commitment to Christ to serve the poor. She was over sixty years of age, blind, and she walked hunched over. What could this woman do with these limitations? But she had never been bothered by limitations. Blinded as an infant, she began writing poems early in life and came to the attention of the public. In *Favorite Hymn Writers* (Westchester, Ill.: Good News Publishers, Crossway Books, 1990), James Stuart Smith and Betty Carlson record that:

> In 1843 Fanny Crosby went to Washington, D.C., with other blind friends to prove to government leaders that blind people can be educated if they have the proper training. The first woman ever to speak before the Senate, she moved many senators to tears with her poems and winning personality.

She knew Presidents John Tyler, John Quincy Adams, and Grover Cleveland, and she often opened Congress with one of her poems.

She was a friend of Dwight L. Moody and his song leader, Ira D. Sankey. Many of her poems had been put to music, and she was already known as an outstanding hymn writer. The Chattauqua Society listed her as their poet laureate. She, at age sixty, was a Christian celebrity, if in the late 1800s there was such a thing. Now Mrs. Van Alsyne, better known as Fanny J. Crosby, writer of over three thousand poems and hymns, was to become Aunt Fanny, mission worker.

Fanny moved into a tenement building and sold three hymns a week at $2.00 per hymn. She then dedicated her time to working at the Bowery Mission, the McAuley Water Street Mission, the Door of Hope (for women), and other skid row mission works. She spoke at YMCAs, churches, and prisons. It was at a prison that a man yelled out, "Good Lord! Do not pass me by." That evening she wrote, "Pass Me Not Oh Gentle Savior." During this period some of her best-loved hymns were written. They include: "Blessed Assurance," "He Hideth My Soul," "I Am Thine O Lord," "Jesus Is Tenderly Calling Me Home," "To God Be the Glory," "Jesus Keep Me Near the Cross," and the home-mission favorite, "Rescue the Perishing." It became the battle cry for rescue missions and other outreaches to the lost and broken.

What could a blind senior citizen, alone and hunched over, do to be salt and light in the Bowery of New York? Fanny went into the mission halls and would sniff out the worst smelling man and sit next to him. She called this conversational evangelism. Each man was one of "her" boys, and she loved them to Jesus. It was one night as one of those boys went forward that she wrote "Rescue the Perishing." The words from the second verse express Fanny's heart for the lost and broken:

> Rescue the perishing, Care for the dying,
> Snatch them in pity from sin and the grave;
> Weep o'er the erring one, Lift up the fallen,
> Tell them of Jesus, the mighty to save.
> Down in the human heart, Crushed by the tempter,
> Feelings lie buried that Grace can restore.
> Touched by a loving heart, Wakened by kindness
> Cords that were broken will vibrate once more.
> Rescue the perishing, Care for the dying;
> Jesus is merciful, Jesus will save.

On occasion, when Fanny Crosby was to open the United States Senate in Washington with one of her new poems, she became worried because the session was starting late. She approached the presiding officer and said, "If you don't get these boys quieted down, I'm going to have to leave, for my boys at the mission need me more than you do."

Fanny spent the last years of her life in Bridgeport, Connecticut, living with relatives and ministering regularly at the Bridgeport Christian Union. She continued well into her eighties, visiting mission ministries throughout the east. Her simple grave marker is in the shadow of the monument for P. T. Barnum, the circus magnate. His monument is large and ostentatious and her's small and simple. It says:

> Fanny J. Crosby
> "Aunt Fanny"
> She did what she could.

Fanny Crosby had nothing to offer to a mission except her love, her hope, her motherly care. She had no training to work with alcoholics, prostitutes, and drug addicts. She was just a simple woman who became salt and light to hundreds of society's forgotten people. All who work with the poor long for more like Aunt Fanny who do what they can.

> If I have the gift of prophecy and can fathom all mysteries and all knowledge, and if I have a faith that can move mountains, but have not love, I am nothing (1 Cor. 13:2).

Quotes

Smith and Carlson include a quote of Fanny Crosby's philosophy of living.

> You can't save a man by telling him of his sins. He knows them already. Tell him there is a pardon and love waiting for him. . . . Make him understand you believe in him, and never give up.

Bernard Ruffin includes a number of Fanny Crosby's insightful comments in *Fanny Crosby* (Cleveland, Ohio: United Church Press), 1976.

> A neighbor in the tenement where Fanny Crosby lived said, "If I had wealth I would be able to do just what I wish to do; . . . and I would be able to make an appearance in the world." Fanny said, "Well, take the world but give me Jesus."

Take the world, but give me Jesus, All its joys are but a name,
But His love abideth ever, Through eternal years the same.

A great many people sympathize with me, . . . but although
I am grateful to them, I really don't need their sympathy.
What would I do with it? . . . You see, I was blind from the
time I was six weeks old and I never knew what it was to see
with my eyes. Yet when I was six years old I could climb a
tree like a squirrel and ride a horse bare-back.

Do not let go to decay and ruin those vast interior regions
of thought and feeling, good brother or sister! Your memory
would be much to you if you were ever deprived of some of
the organs of sense that so distract you from deep and continued thought.

While in deep depression, Fanny cried out to the Lord,

Dear Lord hold my hand! . . . Almost at once, the sweet
peace that comes of perfect assurance returned to my heart,
and my gratitude for the evidence of answered prayer sang
itself into the lines of the hymn:

> Hold Thou my hand, so weak am I and helpless,
> I dare not take one step without Thy aid;
> Hold Thou my hand, for then, oh, loving Savior,
> No dread of ill shall make my soul afraid.

From the time I received the first check for my poems, I
made up my mind to open my hand wide to those who needed
assistance.

I could give more than one instance where men have been
reclaimed, after a long struggle and many attempts at
reformation, because someone spoke a kind word to them,
even, at what appeared to be the last moment. I have also known
many others who turned away from a meeting simply because
the cheering word had not been spoken, nor the helping hand
extended. Never chide the erring has been my policy, for I
firmly believe that harsh words only serve to harden hearts
that might otherwise be softened into repentance.

Not one of them was ever ugly to me. . . . If they are bad,
then poor souls, they need help all the more. . . . Love counts
more than anything else. It is wonderful!

During twenty-five years in mission-work, I have seen those of whom you could say, "Why, we cannot do any-thing." You don't know what you can do until you try. I have sat down by people who had no hope, and yet that divine principle of love was brought to them, and they have wept tears.

———— 6 ————

God Is Love

George & Sarah Clarke

. . . A few signs painted on the walls. One of them, centered halfway across the front, read GOD IS LOVE. . . . Night after night thieves, harlots and alcoholics were loosed from Satan's chains and wooed through the Clarkes' ministry into the loving heart of God. . . . [Billy] Sunday was under tremendous conviction. Mother Clarke came back to his side and said, putting her arm around Billy, "Young man, God loves you. Jesus died for you, and He wants you to love Him and give your heart to Him." The ball player could no longer resist.

—Carl F. H. Henry

Introduction

*S*arah Dunn Clarke wrote the first history of the Pacific Garden Mission, in Chicago, and titled it, "God Is Love." Sarah wrote:

I was born November 13, 1835 in Cayuga County, New York—had the advantages of Sunday school, and from youth, longed to become a Christian (having no knowledge of cards, theaters, or the dance) but no one ever asked me personally about the interests of my soul until the year 1855. When returning from Wilkes Barre Seminary with a friend, while on the platform of Scranton Depot, about to separate, asked me if I would "give my heart to God." I then and there—said I would, which was the beginning of my Christian life. . . . A few years later . . . I received a God-given message controlling the whole trend of my future life. I was faithful in all my church relations, but never knew the value of consecrated time—until the completion of an elaborate piece of work for the decoration of our family home, when an audible voice seemed to speak from heaven, saying: "What are you doing to decorate your heavenly home?"

This soul-penetrating question so impressed me with time's sacred value—God's precious time—God's price-less time, being spent on earthly adornments that would perish—when souls won for the Master would adorn the Heavenly Mansion through all the cycles of eternity.

The recognition of this stupendous fact, placed such a premium on time—such a value on souls—that it at once became the all absorbing and consuming passion of my life, and the agencies that have been set in motion, are still multiplying their influences in the world today—that will live—on and on—yes on—and—on—forever.

Moving to Chicago a few years later, I supposed that I must conform to city customs, but when trying to make so-called "fashionable" calls, I began to remonstrate with my conscience in spending time so unsatisfactory—it seemed so perfunctory—only an empty void.

Sarah probably was looking into the mirror admiring her beautiful dress and may have been ready to put on her ornate hat, when her eyes met her reflection. Like many other women, she wondered, *What am I doing with my life?* Her own question so gripped her that

> . . . changing my attire [I] visited some poor families and
> in ministering to their needs found such a real soul satisfac-
> tion—such a consciousness of God's approval—that I was at
> once convinced my mission in life had been revealed.

What met Sarah Dunn's eyes that day had to be terrifying, and
only through the power of the Holy Spirit could she continue. The
Civil War had left the northern cities in a chaotic state. So many
men had died in the war leaving widows and orphans. War and prostitution went hand in hand. Sarah visited families that were holding
on with moral courage. They were poor before the war; now their
poverty was wringing out the hope that they had. Mothers clung to
their children, dressed in pitiful gray rags that matched the gray circles
under their desperate eyes.

Large numbers of people, both black and white, young and old,
flowed up North from the devastated South, some to forget their
troubles, others to find a new life.

> After, having a large number of poor families on my list,
> [I] joined with others in starting a mission Sunday school in
> 1869 at the corner of State and Twenty-Third Streets.

Sarah walked the filthy, crime-filled streets among the diseased
and dying, but she brought a touch of God's love into the lives of
hopeless individuals.

The mission Sunday school was a warm, loving, safe place where a
child could be a child. There was laughter, singing, Bible verses, and
so on. For many it was an escape from the horror of their lives into
the loving arms of Jesus. Sarah not only "let the little children come"
(Mark 10:14) to Jesus, she took them by the hand and with words
and deeds led them to the Savior.

Colonel George R. Clarke met Sarah while she was running the
mission Sunday school. He knew exactly what he was getting into
when he married her—she was a woman with a passion for the poor
as a consuming commitment was developing in her heart. George
and Sarah were married on a stormy winter day, January 23, 1873.
He helped her a little in the mission Sunday school, but it wasn't as
deep in his heart and soul as it was in his wife's.

When the Chicago fire roared through the city, it burned down
churches and "dens of iniquity" all in one giant inferno. Quickly the
saloons, the brothels, and the gambling halls rebuilt. The sordid
businesses put up their little shacks, but not the church.[1] Even the
great evangelist Dwight L. Moody did not move back because the fire

instilled such a fear in his wife she refused to move back. In the midst of the desolation, Sarah managed to continue to minister to people with physical and spiritual needs. She realized more was needed than visiting families and conducting the weekly mission Sunday school. Something had to be done for desperate men and women who roamed the streets. The only places they had to turn to were the brothels, saloons, and opium dens. She wanted them to know the Savior and His love. Her heart beat with compassion for children and poor families. There needed to be a united mission, and she started pleading with God.[2] Her husband wasn't sure about that one, no not at all! God, however, in His great way moves in the hearts of individuals. We can't understand; it is not in our human understanding, and yet the Spirit moves on the hearts of individuals in the most dramatic ways.

Before the Civil War, George Clarke had studied law and was admitted to the bar, but he soon realized he could make money in real estate.

> On the eve of participating in a questionable business trans-
> action—providence divinely interposed through the remem-
> brance of his sainted Mother's prayers, not only awakening
> his conscience to the penalty of such a transgression, but the
> enormity of sin in God's sight, so convicting him—his pur-
> pose was averted. With great agony of conscience he repented
> before the Lord until he had the assurance of forgiveness
> through the divine atonement of the Lord Jesus Christ.[3]

It wasn't until many years later he was ready to make a business deal in Colorado that would make him and Sarah wealthy. The Spirit once again took hold of his heart:

> "Oh God, you know I love you and I want to do what is
> right and good in your sight. You know what a mess I make
> of preaching and how my heart aches for the miserable people
> dear Sarah wants to reach. Show me, oh Lord, what must I
> do and give me the power to do your blessed will."[4] He tele-
> graphed his wife of his change of life purposes and added
> that he was returning to Chicago at once to join her in found-
> ing a mission.[5]

Oh, how happy Sarah was when she received the telegram. It had been six years from the time that she had first received the vision for a united mission. She knew the two of them could hand-in-hand serve the Lord. Relief, peace, and joy filled Sarah's heart. George found her easier to live with as God blessed their marriage. They were now in the battle together overcoming evil with good.

The neglected masses found refuge as they walked through the open doors of the rescue mission.

> We held the fort—Mr. Clarke preached—and I tried to keep crooked men straight. But such coming and going was never seen before. Order—heaven's "first law"—had never been injected in their minds and it took the wisdom of Solomon to separate the drunken men and keep that crowd in order.[6]

They soon needed more space and the colonel found just what they wanted. The Pacific Beer Garden's lease was up for sale. It was known as the most notorious, murderous joint west of New York City. Not long after the mission moved, Dwight L. Moody suggested they "strike out the 'beer' and add the word mission."

When the mission adopted by-laws, the purpose was "to hold and conduct religious services, to carry on and conduct public meetings, to furnish food, lodging and assistance to the needy and unfortunate, and to do religious and benevolent work of all kinds."

> After the Clarkes leased for God the area once occupied by the notorious Pacific Beer Garden, they threw themselves into the work with even greater ardor, resulting in an endless stream of gloriously transformed lives. They never had children of their own, but, in a real sense, these were their children. Many of them in later years tenderly called Mrs. Clarke "mother."[7] For thirty-five years after the mission's founding, Mother Clarke was the great heart of love that moved its hands. After the first fifteen years, in 1892, Colonel Clarke died. All the more she felt the challenge to carry on with a double task.[8]

Conclusion

Today the Pacific Garden Mission is massive, and it produces the radio program *Unshackled*, which is broadcast all over the world.

Endnotes

1. Sarah D. Clarke, *The Founding of Pacific Garden Mission, God Is Love* (Chicago: The Bronson Canode Printing Co, 1914), 17.

2. Carl F. H. Henry, *The Pacific Garden Mission* (Grand Rapids: Zondervan Publishing House, 1942), p. 27.
3. Clarke, *God Is Love*, 14–15.
4. James R. Adair, *The Old Lighthouse* (Chicago: Moody Press, 1966), 31–32.
5. Henry, *Pacific Garden Mission*, 27.
6. Clarke, *God Is Love*, 20.
7. Adair, *The Old Lighthouse*, 37.
8. Henry, *Pacific Garden Mission*, 79.

Rescue Us from the Present Evil

Eva von Tiele-Winckler

[Christ] gave himself for our sins to rescue us from the present evil.
—Galatians 1:3–4

All over the world this gospel is bearing fruit and growing, just as it has been doing among you since the day you heard it and understood God's grace in all its truth.
—Colossians 1:6

Introduction

$\mathcal{E}$ very fly in India seemed to be swirling around our heads. The continual odor from raw sewage filled our noses. Our sister in the Lord, who is a city missionary, led the way as her sari flowed over her shoulder. The City Mission World Association Committee was on its way to see one of her visions that had become a reality—an orphanage for children. Recent riots had left two more children orphaned. We visited five slums and met twenty-seven of her Christian workers who lived in them.

That evening we talked over our trip into the slums. We rejoiced with what God's love had done through one woman. Members of the committee from different continents started telling about women who worked in their missions.

One of the members of the committee was Dr. Paul Toaspern, a wise Christian man from the former DDR (East Germany). He has lived under Naziism and Communism. The Christians ran fourteen city missions, forty-two hospitals, three hundred homes for the elderly, and ninety-two mental hospitals. The communists had said, "If you Christians are dumb enough to take care of these people, go right ahead. They cannot contribute to the state."[1] As we were talking, I asked Dr. Toaspern, "Was there a woman in the DDR that inspired the Christians to reach out to the poor?" "Yes," he said. "I rewrote a book on her life for the people. Her name was Mother Eva."

Eva was born in 1866 into a wealthy Prussian (German) family who lived in a castle. Her mother died when Eva was young, and her father was gone much of the time because he was in the military. She wrote,

> When I was seventeen, being alone in my little room, it pleased the Lord Jesus to reveal Himself to me in a sudden and remarkable way, so that I was changed in a moment from an unbeliever without knowledge of salvation into a follower of Christ. At the same time He who is love poured into my heart a deep love for the poor and forsaken ones, and gave me a vivid impression of the great need.[2]

She read the gospel of John and discovered the words of the Good Shepherd (John 10:1–18). She prayed, "Oh Lord, if you really are the Good Shepherd, then you shall be my shepherd and my life belongs to you. . . . I want to serve you with all my heart and live for the poor."[3]

Soon she was visiting the poor in the village, giving out food, clothing, medicine, and the Gospel. She went into the tiny, disease-infested huts and tried to soothe the sick, hold the babies, and bring a little laughter. All of this was against her father's wishes. An aristocrat, he had raised his daughter not to mingle with the lower class.

After prodding her, he recognized that he would not change his daughter's mind so he built her a cottage to house six needy people. Before long she had forty. As he saw her at work, his heart was eventually softened and he gave money and property to the ministry.

Eva started a deaconess movement and they called themselves sisters. We're all sisters and brothers when we share the Lord Jesus Christ and are sensitive to each other's hurts and needs. When the world sees us display that kind of love, then they will know us by our love.

> Love one another. As I have loved you, so you must love one another. By this all men will know that you are my disciples if you love one another (John 13:34–35).

The few women who joined her lived together, and they gave their money away, learning to live by faith, following Jesus. These were hard times; there was a great depression, then war. The sisters attended the Welsh Revival of 1905 and were filled with the Holy Spirit in a powerful way. They had joy in the midst of the despair. By God's grace they grew in number to eight hundred single women for ministry, and the deaconesses used the Bible as their guide. "The precedent for this ministry is found in the early church where women such as Phoebe (mentioned in Romans 16:1) carried out a ministry of service (diakonia)."[4] The need was great, and they opened forty orphanages, housing over two thousand orphans.[5] Little children often suffered the most during war, and women often turned to prostitution or were forced into it. Mother Eva opened rescue homes for them and her deaconesses became hospital nurses and foreign missionaries.

The hours were long, the work hard, but Mother Eva still found time to write poems and keep a diary. These were the thoughts that Dr. Toaspern felt needed to be shared with the Christians who lived under communism, especially the women. The young people needed to know how God works in the lives of individuals and uses them in difficult situations. Eva's life continues to give encouragement—encouragement to the seventeen-year-old girl who says, "I'm miserable. I have a nice house, but my mom is never home and my dad is always at work. Does anyone really care about me?" Yes, Jesus really cares, whether you live in a castle or in extreme poverty.

Eva lived in an evil time and yet was rescued, and she rescued and inspired others even after her death in 1930. Ten of her sisters joined Hudson Taylor at the China Inland Mission in opening China for the Gospel. The work continued through Hitler and then under communism, and over six hundred sisters are still at work today helping the poor. Eva, this Protestant saint, has served as an inspiration for city missionaries for over one hundred years and truly was a mother of a great movement that brought thousands of women into service to God, evangelizing and serving the poor and most needy.

Endnotes

1. Paul Toaspern, interview with Delores Burger.
2. Ernest Gordon, quoting Eva von Winckler in *A Book of Protestant Saints* (Grand Rapids: Zondervan Publishing House, 1940), 85.
3. Toaspern, interview.
4. Reid, Linder, Shelly, and Stout, eds., *Dictionary of Christianity in America*, (InterVarsity Press, 1990), 334.
5. Gordon, *Protestant Saints*, 85.

8

Rescue the Poor Who Cry for Help

Annie Green

God in his infinite wisdom prepares and trains a particular individual by using . . . heritage and the circumstances of every day life to bring his compassion, practical help and salvation into areas of need and neglect. Annie Green was literally impelled by the love of Christ, not for a short-term project but for a ministry which spanned nearly sixty years. . . . As seen against a colorful backdrop interwoven from the strands which make up the history of South Australia.

—Esther Green

Introduction

*T*he history of city missions in Australia is the history of colonization in Australia. It is clear to me that God has used women, in the midst of social upheaval and war, to proclaim His truth as they "rescued the poor who cry for help" (Job 29:12). Looking back, we see the mighty hand of God working in circumstances that are difficult to understand now. Annie Green was one of these women. The source for this information is a book by Esther Green, *Evergreen Annie: The Life of Annie Green of the Adelaide City Mission, 1858–1936* (Adelaide, Australia: Adelaide City Mission, 1988).

She was born in 1858 to a hardworking colonial family near Melbourne, in Brunswick, Australia, during the Victorian gold rush. Her father was a butcher. Annie as a teenager attended her best friend's church, where she professed Christ as Savior. Her testimony is truly great! Every family has heartaches, and when Annie's sister became pregnant by a seminary student, there were lots of tears. The family thought it best to move, and they chose Adelaide, South Australia.

In 1867, the Adelaide City Mission was formed by a Scot who had worked in missions there. Programs were started, including an evening Sunday school and an English school for two hundred Chinese who lived near the mission. At the age of twenty-two, Annie became the mission's female missionary and her title became Agent Annie Green.

> Her "qualifications" being a good voice, the ability to play the piano, a commanding personality, willingness to assist the poor and needy and the very love of Christ for the wayward.

Unmarried men outnumbered women by three thousand in Adelaide, and although women could get work as midwives, laundresses, dress-makers, or nurses, many became prostitutes. The mission was in the heart of the red-light district. Annie's compassion went out to these women as she suffered with them. Some chose prostitution as a way of life; others had, like her sister, become pregnant but didn't have a family who stood with them. They were branded as fallen women and thrown out of the families, the churches, and the community.

Annie didn't see them as outcasts, and with a mother's heart she became committed to rescuing these women. They could become strong women, hard working citizens, and godly wives and mothers.

She did her rescue work at midnight, and with a few of her female friends, Annie formed the Night Rescue Association, using the mission's facilities.

This sort of work, walking the streets, hanging around brothels and accosting strange young women who were soliciting was not for the chicken-hearted. Annie was only twenty-five herself when she commenced with other team members, both men and women, an effort which would have required physical and moral courage as well as an intense love for these girls and a desire for their highest welfare.

Newcomers were the most vulnerable and efforts were now made to prevent the entrapping of young women arriving in the colony from England. The Night Rescue Association had cards printed, and distributed in England by the Y.W.C.A. to all single female emigrants upon embarkation. These cards directed the girls where to go for a free night's lodging and breakfast next morning. This was an attempt to thwart their being drawn into the brothels (posing as rooming houses) as soon as they landed at Port Adelaide and were approached by "operators."

Annie Green's experience in preaching, organizing relief and counseling was gained year by year in the harness of her calling. In 1923 as a proven administrator, organizer, and preacher, she was appointed the General Superintendent of the A.C.M. [Adelaide City Mission], the first woman in Australia—in Protestant circles at least—to hold such a position. She it was who guided the Mission's programs through a Second Depression and was an adviser to the Premier, Sir Richard Butler.

As the city changed, Annie, with a mother's heart, started or revised programs. She started homes for women and children, employment programs, boys and girls clubs, and more. She advised her youth workers:

Make the meeting as interesting as you can. Remember that the children have undeveloped minds and you will have to counteract their home environment. Bring the Lord into it gradually, in such a way that they will accept the fact that He is in the Mission and in you. Convey to them what a wonderful thing it is to know the Lord.

The Gospel was the center of her work, which spanned sixty years. She was seventy-seven when she died.

A Tribute to Miss Annie Green

Miss Annie Syrette Green, the greatly beloved Superintendent of the Adelaide City Mission, died last night. . . . She
gave her life to the poorest the lowliest and the lost. For years
she has been struggling to carry on in spite of great physical
disabilities, because her love for her work was her life. . . .
Many thousands in this state have been given their new beginning through her selfless work of love (The *News* 4 16,
1936).

God knows the change of governments, boundaries, countries,
and economies. In His great love, He saw the needs of the poor of
Australia and provided Annie to be a great, godly leader. He is now
preparing and calling those to do rescue work in new locations as we
head toward 2000 and beyond.

And we have seen and testify that the Father has sent his
Son to be the Savior of the world. If anyone acknowledges
that Jesus is the Son of God, God lives in him and he in God.
And so we know and rely on the love God has for us. God is
love (1 John 4:14–16).

Such was the life of Annie. The Adelaide City Mission continues
to this day, and its symbol is a red heart. What a fitting remembrance
of Annie Green, who truly became the heart of that great city!

---- *9* ----

Undivided Devotion

Anne Spellman   Mamie Caskie   Jennie Goranflo

> *. . . He that is unmarried careth for the things that belong to the Lord, and how he may please the Lord: But he that is married careth for the things that are of the world, how he may please his wife. . . . The unmarried woman careth for the things of the Lord, that she may be holy both in body and in spirit: but she that is married careth for the things of the world, how she may please her husband.*
> —*1 Corinthians 7:33–34 KJV*

> *I am saying this for your own good, not to restrict you, but that you may live in a right way in undivided devotion to the Lord.*
> —*1 Corinthians 7:36*

Introduction

*T*he apostle Paul talks about being single as an advantage to serving God, especially during difficult times. Historically, groups of men and women have remained single in both Catholic and Protestant traditions. Others have not been part of a group but have sacrificed to serve, giving their lives totally to God.

Forsaking All Others

Campers gathered at Walnutport Camp Meeting noticed a fine carriage drawn by two beautiful horses. . . . It was Grandfather coming with an ultimatum for his granddaughter Anne. "Come with me now; forget this religion; or you will no longer be welcomed in our home." The heart breaking decision was made. Grandfather left alone.[1]

> Encamped along the hills of light, Ye Christian soldiers rise,
> And press the battle ere the night shall veil the glowing skies,
> Against the foe in vales below, Let all our strength be hurled;
> Faith is the victory, we know, That overcomes the world.
> Faith is the victory! Faith is the victory!
> Oh, glorious victory, That overcomes the world.
> —John H. Yates

From that moment on, twenty-two-year-old Miss Anne Spellman trusted the Lord to guide her. She became a district leader in the Gospel Workers Society. Twenty years later the Lord called her to Detroit, Michigan, where she founded the Missionary Workers Society Interdenominational, made up of single women. They branched out into other cities establishing missions. Angela Phipps became a strong leader in Chicago well into the 1970s.

Some of their missions became churches and one became a Bible school. Their mission in Detroit was sold to the Detroit Rescue Mission Ministries in 1987. It is amazing how God's plan has unfolded. When we visited the Detroit Rescue Mission, the old Missionary Workers Tabernacle walls vibrated as over one hundred staff members, black and white, sang and testified to the power of God. It can be said of them as it was said of Anne Spellman, "Many were won by observing the love of God shining on her face."

Grace and Hope for All

It was during the momentous summer of 1914, just prior to the beginning of World War I, that two missionaries, Mamie E. Caskie and Jennie E. Goranflo, felt led of the Lord to come to Baltimore, Maryland . . . to open a Gospel Mission. They had seventeen years of experience in mission work with the Gospel Workers Society of Cleveland, Ohio, a great faith in God and $13 in money . . . so with just enough money to rent a room at the YWCA and $4 in cash, but claiming the promise in Philippians 4:19, "But my God shall supply all your need according to his riches in glory by Christ Jesus" [KJV] they started out.[2]

Their object: "to rescue the lost, help the poor and needy, visit the sick and dying." Their motto: "Grace and hope for all." Eighty-one years later, eleven Grace and Hope Missions in seven eastern states, operated completely by single women missionaries, continue that vision.

Beyond the Call of Duty
Often single women working for a male director went far beyond the call of duty due to dedication and availability, usually with no recognition or accolades. One such worker shared:

I did everything. If somebody got married, I had to fill that job. I did secretarial work, I worked with the women's programs, I worked with the children up at camp. . . . I was really the assistant superintendent but . . . he would never publicly announce it. . . . He would say, "You're my right-hand man" . . . but he would never admit my role as his assistant.[3]

A few months ago we walked into a mission lobby and were greeted by a single woman, "Hello, I'm the desk man today." That ministry is going through a crisis and she is holding it together until the board hires a new director.

Dr. W. E. Paul wrote in *Romance of Rescue:*

A survey showed more than fifty missions operated by women as Superintendents, and among them are some of the very best missions in our country. The place of women in Gospel and Rescue Missions has generally been an inconspicuous one, but it would be a great mistake to draw the conclusion that their work has been any less effective than that of men.[4]

Like a mighty army, single women marched on the cities of

America. They founded and built the Olive Branch Mission, in Chicago, Illinois; the Waterfront Mission in Pensacola, Florida; South Side Mission in Peoria, Illinois, to name a few. Single women founded the Gospel Mission Workers, the Missionary Workers Society Interdenominational, the Grace and Hope Missions, and of course, so many of the famous Salvation Army women were unmarried. Often without fanfare, they changed the face of America's cities.

And the story continues. . . . Single women are at the forefront today in starting women and family shelters, pregnancy homes, and inner-city youth ministries. They are often the only ones willing to live in inner-city family shelters.

Today we need more single women, young and old, for they have the advantage of being able to serve God with undivided devotion in places of danger and need. If God is calling you, don't let others talk you out of His plan for your life. Catherine Booth, cofounder of the Salvation Army, wrote:

> Not she with traitorous lips her Savior stung,
> Not she denied Him with unholy tongue:
> She, whilst apostles shrunk, could danger brave;
> Last at the cross, and earliest at the grave.[5]

Endnotes

1. *God Planned Her Life* (The Mission Workers Society Interdenominational), 4.
2. *Grace and Hope Publication*, October 1989: 5.
3. Virginia Brainard Kunz, *Where the Doors Never Close* (St. Paul: Union Gospel Mission), 62–63.
4. William E. Paul, *Romance of Rescue* (Minneapolis: Osterhus, 1959), 50–51.
5. Catherine Booth, *Practical Religion* (London: The Salvation Army, 1883), 114.

10

𝒜 𝒨other's 𝒫rayer: 𝒮he 𝒩ever 𝒢ave 𝒰p

Emily & Mel Trotter

I never got so drunk or so far away that I could not always feel the hand of my mother. One of the prettiest things I ever looked at was an old, old hand, all twisted up with rheumatism—the hand of my mother. When my mother lay dying, she turned to me and said, "You win all the souls you can for Jesus and I will see you over there."

—Mel Trotter

Introduction

*T*here was this constant charge of words going back and forth—
of praise, hallelujah, discouragement, encouragement. One
man said how Satan had tempted him to get angry and that God
delivered him. They all shouted, "Hallelujah! Brother!" Another told
of a song of victory he had written in the middle of the night and he
taught us all to sing it.

We all sat at the table, eating our scrambled eggs and bacon around
the mission's breakfast table. Steve and I were surrounded by eight
disciples—twenty to thirty-year-old black men who were in the long-
term recovery/discipleship program at the mission. Never before had
I sat with a group of Christians that were charged with the power of
God like these young men. They would use that power—that song—
that victory in just a few minutes outside the walls of the mission,
reaching the city for Christ.

"What brought you to the mission?" I asked each one.

"I was laying out on the street. I was a mess and God said, 'Go to
that mission. They will help you.'" Another said, "My grandmother's
prayers." But most said, "My mother's prayers brought me here."
The power of a mother's prayers that blends her love with the love of
God reaches deep and long into a heart. Mothers of prodigals, take
courage! Many prayers have been answered!

～⊙～

It is amazing how God has a master plan for each one of our lives
and how our lives touch each other, and it's not until we can look
back that we understand the plan of the almighty God. This plan
keeps unfolding from century to century. In 1842 Emily Lorch was
born in Springfield, Illinois. A little friend who lived next door was
named Anna Herdon, and her daddy was a law partner of Abraham
Lincoln. So Emily knew Abraham Lincoln and saw him often. There's
so much history in this little girl's life that you can follow.

Emily met and married William Trotter at the end of the Civil
War. They moved to Orangeville, Illinois, and Mel Trotter was born
on May 16, 1870. When Mel was five years old they moved to Polo,
Illinois, which was in the center of a farming area. Emily had such a
hard life married to William because he was a habitual drunkard.
Today we'd call him an alcoholic, but back then they said *drunkard*.
He earned his living as a bartender, and he and Emily had seven
children. Mel ran the streets, he didn't go to school, and he got in
trouble. His mother tried her best; she did teach her children how to
pray, "Now I lay me down to sleep, I pray the Lord my soul to
keep. . . ." But William's drinking was too much for Emily. She kept

trying, however. This chapter centers around Emily with the hope it will touch other women in whose lives alcohol has become a difficult part of the marriage.

Mel's parents wanted him to go to school and get an education, but that isn't what Mel wanted. He ran wild. He liked spending time at his father's saloon and gambling—one could say that Mel was following in the footsteps of his father. The whiskey and the gambling took hold of Mel, and for long periods of time he was gone. His mother didn't know where he was, but no matter how far he went or how deeply he got into trouble, he carried his mother's prayers in his heart and would remember them often. What Emily wanted for her children is what Christian mothers want for their children, for them to grow up to serve the Lord, to know Him and live their lives pleasing God. That was not what Mel was doing. His life was a mess. Every time Emily got word about him, it was always bad news. He just went down, down, down, and every report was one that broke her heart. She would cry—cry out to God. She felt that her life was just so painful, and yet she had Jesus. She had fallen in love with a man, and he was a drunk, but now her son was falling into the same pattern. Emily is described as a saintly mother, and she shed many tears for Mel. She kept praying for him, and he said that his mother's prayers always followed him, even when he was in the worst condition.

Later on, Mel was to say, "I never got so drunk or so far away that I could not always feel the hand of my mother." How were her prayers answered? Mel had sunk low, and he no longer liked himself. He had done so many evil things and knew he was living a life that he didn't want to live any more. One cold night in Chicago, Mel was thrown out of a bar and was ready to end his life. He wasn't even wearing a pair of shoes. As he walked by the Pacific Garden Mission on his way to end his life, he was literally pushed in the front door by a mission convert eager to help this desolate young man. Harry Monroe, superintendent of Pacific Garden Mission, was so taken with the condition of Mel that he stopped the evening service, walked down, and prayed for Mel as he was sleeping in a chair. Harry went on with the service and was gratified to find Mel at the altar to receive Christ. After spending several years at the mission, Mel went to Grand Rapids, Michigan, to help a group of Christian men start a rescue mission there. From that place, he reached out and started sixty-seven rescue missions and traveled America as a well-known evangelist. Those missions include Saginaw, Muskegon, and Detroit, Michigan Ft. Wayne, Indiana, and many others.

Yes, a mother's prayers were answered. She lived to see Mel become the Christian man she had prayed for. She lived to see all her children become Christian. Her three sons all became ministers. Mel had another mother, however. That was Mother Clarke, cofounder of Pacific Garden Mission. She mothered Mel when he was away from home. Mother Clarke loved him, encouraged him—they wrote letters back and forth for many years. So here were these two mothers—one never had children of her own, but Mel became like a son. And Mel's mother. Emily had a hard life married to a difficult man, and yet it is because of that very background, I believe, that Mel threw his whole heart and life into the work of rescue. He knew what it was like to be rescued and spent his life rescuing others.

As Mel gave his testimony through the years, the people who were thrilled the most were the people who were drunk or on drugs and far from home—those were the ears that loved to hear his testimony, because then they could find the way out of the mess their lives had become.

Everlastingly at It was Mel's slogan, but it certainly fit his mother. She never gave up on her son—never. "She kept on praying to the Lord" (1 Sam. 1:12).

The Ninety & Nine

There were ninety and nine that safely lay
In the shelter of the fold;
But one was out on the hills away,
Far off from the gates of gold,
Away on the mountain wild and bare,
Away from the tender Shepherd's care,
Away from the tender Shepherd's care.
And all through the mountain, thunder riven
And up from the rocky steep,
There rose a cry to the gates of heaven,
"Rejoice, I have found My sheep!"
And the angels echoed around the throne,
"Rejoice, for the Lord brings back His own,
Rejoice, for the Lord brings back His own."
—Elizabeth C. Clephane

Conclusion

How does this life touch our lives? The mission where I started had on the wall in great big letters Mel's slogan—*Everlastingly at It.* Then there was another slogan—*How long since you wrote to mother?* Missions no longer have that on their walls, because many kids are running away from mothers that mistreat them—not just fathers. The truth is, though, there are many prodigals in mission chapels today. The hope is that we can reunite them with their families. That happens often, like it did with Mel. But every once in awhile we have a funeral for someone who died and we don't have any way to find the family—we don't know whose child he or she is. Sometimes those people have come to know the Lord and are going to spend eternity with Him. I have wondered, "Are they the ones whose moms prayed for them? Are they the ones whose moms never gave up?" It's great to reunite families here on earth. I know there will also be a glorious reuniting when we all get to heaven.

The Master does have a master plan. Emily put her hurt in the hands of almighty God, and I know her prayers had a part in Mel's salvation and reformed life.

> He shall feed his flock like a shepherd: he shall gather the lambs with his arm, and carry them in his bosom, and shall gently lead those that are with young (Isaiah 40:11 KJV).

Additional Reading

Melvin E. Trotter, *These Forty Years* (Grand Rapids: Zondervan Publishing House, 1939).

IUGM, *Rescue Magazine*, 1993: Fall, Summer.

Fred C. Zarfas, *Mel Trotter, A Biography* (Grand Rapids: Zondervan Publishing House, 1950).

11

Compassion

Maude Benton

Because she spent so much time in intercessory prayer and her compassion was so Christlike, Maude Benton was "always loving some mother's son or daughter into the arms of Jesus," many whom others for a long time had given up on. She could see hope for them—hope in Jesus.

When he saw the crowds, he had compassion on them, because they were harassed and helpless, like sheep without a shepherd.
—Matthew 9:36

Introduction

*T*he Christian community held its breath as the great evangelist Dwight L. Moody was overcome by illness and R. A. Torrey
had to complete the crusade (p. 142).[1] "Let not our hearts be troubled,
our Master always has a master plan, and most people who fit in it
are not known by the masses. An evangelistic crusade is like a wed-
ding; the best part is the marriage. It is after the crusade that God's
miracles keep happening."

❧❦❧

Maude Benton had been trained by Moody and Mother Clarke at
the Pacific Garden Mission in Chicago. She was at Moody's last
meeting and he had asked her:

> "Daughter, wouldn't you like to be a Missionary?" He gave
> her a Scripture text, which became her life verse: "He that
> dwelleth in the secret place of the most high shall abide un-
> der the shadow of the Almighty," and the remainder of Psalm
> 91 (page 137).

The crusade over, Maude was like one of the thousands who carried
in their hearts and souls a call on their lives. For most, it was to live
a Christian life. For a few others, it was the call to become
missionaries.

Maude moved to the big city of the west, Los Angeles, and the
first night she was there she found herself sitting in a mission's chapel
service. Mission folks were her Christian family and she felt at home
there. Someone called out, "Can anyone play the piano?" She raised
her hand, and that began her service as a regular volunteer city
missionary, a service which continued for forty-five years at Union
Rescue Mission of Los Angeles, California, until 1952.

> "Some women complain that they can't get along with one
> man," she laughed. "I wonder what they would do with 32!
> I've served under 32 Superintendents here, and I've gotten
> along with all of them (page 140).

She did far more than play the piano. She rode the gospel wagon,
participated in street meetings, served as housemother, clerk, and
counselor. She organized women from thirty-five churches into an
auxiliary. Her sewing day brought out one hundred volunteers. As
needs changed, she could adapt to meet them. During World War
II, the defense plants put to work almost all the men that roamed the

streets. The mission's main program became the Victory Service Club, which served almost two million servicemen (page 143). Maude designed a homemade money belt for servicemen that they could keep their money and family photos in (page 139).

> Whether praying, sewing, listening—whatever the many avenues of contact with the mission, Mother Benton was always loving some mother's son or daughter into the arms of Jesus (page 142).

One of these sons was Bill Stiles who had been a member of the Jesse James and the Younger brothers gangs. He walked into the mission and sat down. As Mother Benton explained:

> I saw one of the men trying to get him to accept Christ, but he wouldn't budge. So I walked back and sat down beside him and asked him if he wouldn't give his heart to the Lord. He jumped up, stepped across me before I could move my feet, and I thought he was going outside to get away from me. Instead, he went running down the aisle and knelt at the altar. I never saw such a change in any man in my life (page 75).

The next day Bill brought to Mother Benton a suitcase full of nitroglycerin that he planned to use in a robbery. She told him they would have to call the police. He agreed. That was his next step back into society, with Mother Benton holding his hand. Bill served the Lord for twenty-four years at the mission and often gave his testimony:

> There is no such thing as reformation for one like me. It takes the power of the Blood of Jesus Christ to blot out transgression and clean one up. Nothing else can take away our sinful appetites and set us free from the power of evil. "He that is free in Christ Jesus is free indeed." . . . Now in place of carrying guns to destroy life, I carry the Word of God that gives life—eternal life (page 77).

When Bill died, he was buried next to Mother Benton's brother. When she visited the cemetery, she tenderly laid flowers on the graves of both her "brothers (page 78)."

Conclusion

The number of homeless people in Los Angeles today is over-whelming. The streets are lined with people, which makes America seem like a lost cause. Yet when we get close and look into their eyes and listen to them, we realize each is an individual created in God's image.

It was just before a street meeting I attended last year at Union Rescue Mission in Los Angeles that I found myself getting to know homeless people one by one. I thought of Mother Benton and re-membered the verse:

> When he saw the crowds, he had compassion on them, because they were harassed and helpless, like sheep without a shepherd (Matt. 9:36).

The testimonies began with a young man speaking in Spanish, then in English. He told how years ago he was eating out of garbage cans, using and selling drugs, then Jesus came into his life. Now he is clean and free, has a job, and even went to South America to start a rescue program. Next an older man got up and asked: "Does any-body remember Mother Benton? She was so kind to me when as a young man I wandered into the mission homeless and hungry. I want the men here to know what God did for me years ago, He can do for you," said Claude Moffatt.

Claude had been touched by Mother Benton, just as she had been influenced by Dwight L. Moody. Claude attended and graduated from the Bible Institute of Los Angeles (BIOLA), became a pastor and denominational leader. He served as the secretary of the Arizona Baptist Association. Under his leadership over one hundred churches were planted.[2] Mother Benton's commitment and compassion lives on through the hundreds she loved and influenced.

Today, as rescue ministries are dealing long term with clients—especially women, children, and younger men—there is an acute need for Mother Bentons—volunteers who can give that extra measure of love, and who can mother and mentor today's outcasts. As the num-bers grow, the number of volunteers must grow if we are going to see the results we desire. The compassion we show today as we volun-teer will bear fruit for years to come.

Endnotes

1. The following quotes are taken from Helga Bender Henry, *Mission on Main Street* (Los Angeles: W. A. Wilde Company, 1955).

2. Michael Teague with Sarah Coleman, *Accomplishing Union Rescue's Mission* (Los Angeles: Union Rescue Mission, 1995), 89.

---- *12* ----

Willing Wife, Willing Widow

Helen & Billy Sunday

Now finish the work, so that your eager willingness to do it may be matched by your completion of it, according to your means.
—*2 Corinthians 8:11*

Now to the unmarried and the widows I say: It is good for them to stay unmarried.
—*1 Corinthians 7:8*

Introduction

*T*here are thousands of willing widows in rescue work around the world. For example, a white-haired grandma came from the country into a crime-filled inner city to become a city missionary. She visited the poor regularly in their homes. They came to love her—the criminals along with the victims of crime. What gave her the courage to have the compassion to become a city missionary? One day this saintly woman looked me square in the eye and said, "Delores, I used to be a 'bar fly.'" Those few words explained it all. She had been rescued. God can use each part of our lives and our husbands' lives to prepare us for His service if we become widows. Helen and Billy Sunday are outstanding examples.

⚜⚜⚜

Helen Amelia Thompson was born into a prosperous family. She learned love in her mother's arms and security in her father's arms. Billy Sunday was born into poverty. He never saw his father, who died during the Civil War. His mother remarried, and Billy, a sickly lad, was sent to a soldier's orphanage by his tearful mother.[1] Helen learned leadership and organizational skills at her church. Billy learned how to play baseball. It took him out of poverty and into fame with the Chicago White Sox. When Helen was twelve, she was led to the Lord by her sixteen-year-old Sunday school teacher. Billy was saved at the Pacific Garden Mission on Chicago's skid row. They met in church. In Billy's words:

> The first time I saw those flashing black eyes and dark hair and white teeth, I said to myself, "There's a swell girl." I always planned to attend that church and the young people's meetings when the club was playing in Chicago.... I used to attend prayer meeting where I could keep one eye on Nell ... and the other on the preacher. Finally, one time I went to see her—it was New Year's night. . . . She had ditched her beau, and I had given the gate to a girl in Iowa. So I braced right up, just before midnight, and asked, "Nell, will you marry me?" She came back so quick it almost floored me. "Yes, with all my heart."[2]

They were married for a few years when with Helen's encouragement, Billy became an evangelist.[3] She organized the crusades, which often included mission testimonies. Billy became America's most famous evangelist between the eras of Dwight L. Moody and Billy Graham. She helped him preach to millions and they dramatically changed America's moral values.[4] The two had become one and they needed each other. Then God had another plan for Helen's life. In her words:

> We had lived together for forty-seven years—we had traveled together for thirty-nine years in the work—and he was gone! . . . I went and knelt down in front of the bed. I put my head on Billy's forearm as he lay there dead, and I said, "Lord, if there's anything left in the world for me to do, if you'll let me know about it. I want to promise you I'll try to do the best I know how." I want to admit to you that I don't see one single thing left for me to do! Billy was my job. . . .[5]

That prayer laid the foundation of willingness that God built Ma Sunday's future ministry on.

> I am thine, O Lord, I have heard thy voice.
> And it told thy love to me;
> But I long to rise in the arms of faith
> And be closer drawn to thee.
> Draw me nearer, nearer, blessed Lord,
> To the cross where thou hast died;
> Draw me nearer, nearer, nearer blessed Lord,
> To thy precious, bleeding side.
> —Fanny Crosby

The widow Sunday was still human. After the funeral, sitting alone in her house, she could listen to the clock ticking. Painful memories filled her mind as she closed her eyes and rested her head on the back of the chair. Billy's body laid in a grave next to their three sons. Daughter Helen was gone, too. All her children and her husband dead! It would be natural to ask, "Why, God? Why? Why am I left?" The painful thoughts about her children . . . if I had only . . . maybe they would not have . . .

Guilt can twist and turn in the mind, trying to get down into the heart. Many widows get mad at God and develop arthritis of the heart. Their hearts are so filled with pain and guilt they can no longer beat with compassion for others. Bitterness takes over and they are robbed of their joy. Not Helen Sunday. She lived out the Scriptures:

> Restore to me the joy of your salvation and grant me a willing spirit, to sustain me (Psalm 51:12).

Be of good courage, and he shall strength your heart, all
ye that hope in the LORD (Psalm 31:24 KJV).

Now it was Helen's turn up to bat and she hit a home run! She had
center stage and all eyes were on her. Her first speaking engagement
as a widow was a great success as it touched many hearts. In her words:

> I got through my message—I had written something to
> say—I didn't exactly read it, but I headed my message,
> "Things I'm thankful for" and I said, "Folks, it's surprising
> how many things God can reveal to you to be thankful for, if
> you really want to know and ask him to help you." I had no
> idea there were so many! But when I prayed and asked God
> to help me write them down, they came into my mind one
> after the other.[6]

She was thankful for rescue missions and often said, "I love them
because that's where my Billy was saved." It had been years before
that

> . . . Mother Clarke came back to his side and said, putting
> her arm around Billy, "Young man, God loves you. Jesus died
> for you, and He wants you to love Him and give your heart
> to Him." . . . Harry Monroe [a mission convert] came to his
> side and they knelt for prayer.[7]

Helen Sunday became "mother" to thousands of rescue mission
workers and converts as she traveled North America from 1935 to
1957.[8] Her suffering allowed her to suffer with others. She could tell
a story as well as Billy, and she could laugh and get others to laugh
with her. The heartache in the cities was massive, fueled by depression and war, and she knew how to minister to heartache. Those she
touched reached out and touched others. The legacy of this willing
widow still lives.

Endnotes

1. Carl F. H. Henry, *The Pacific Garden Mission* (Grand Rapids:
   Zondervan, 1942), 41.
2. "Autobiography of Billy Sunday," *Ladies Home Journal*, 32–33.
3. Opal Cording Overmyer, *Remarkable "Ma" Sunday* (Grand Rapids: Zondervan, 1957), 12.
4. Daniel G. Reid, ed., *Dictionary of Christianity in America*
   (Downers Grove, Ill.: InterVarsity Press, 1990), 1146.

5. *Ma Sunday Still Speaks*, transcription of tape recording (Winona Lake, Ind.: Winona Lake Christian Assembly, 39).
6. Ibid., 41.
7. Henry, *Pacific Garden Mission*, 44.
8. *Our Missions*, October 1940, 11–13.

Bibliography

Rescue, a publication of the IUGM, Kansas City, Missouri, vol. 6, no. 6 (Fall 1992): 3–4.

13

Madams and Pimps

Beulah Bulkley

Then said Jesus . . . "If any man who will come after me, let him deny
himself, and take up his cross, and follow me. For whosoever will save
his life shall lose it: and whosoever will lose his life
for my sake shall find it."

—Matthew 16:24–25 KJV

Introduction

*T*his interview with Beulah Bulkley as told to Laura Rollins Hockaday appeared in the *Kansas City Times*, January 18, 1968.

When my husband told me he wanted to start a mission for the unfortunates of the streets, I told him he was crazy. I wrote a letter to my mama and told her I was going to take our little girl and come home. Mama wrote me back and said, "Ruth is as much your husband's as yours and you better think carefully about leaving." I then became very sick and I was told I would have to have an operation. I was happy because I thought our money would go to pay the doctor bills and there wouldn't be enough to start the mission. My husband came to me in the hospital and threw himself on the bed and cried. He said he had to do what God had called him to do. . . . My heart broke to see him like that. The hours of arguing faded in that instant, and I said if God would give me the strength to regain my health, I would devote my life to my husband's work.

✦✦❀✦✦

The following account is taken from an article by A. B. Macdonald, published in the *Kansas City Star*, February 18, 1934.

To understand how Annie Chambers found God, one must first know the Rev. David Bulkley and his wife and their City Union mission in Kansas City's North Side.

Bulkley is one of those men, rarely met with in these days, who believe Jesus meant it when, in calling His Disciples, He said to them: "Whosoever will come after me let him give all that he hath to the poor, and deny himself and take up his cross and follow me."

"Dave" Bulkley did that. After years of religious work, as a YMCA secretary, preacher and evangelist, having gone overseas with the 1st division in the World War and been wounded in battle in France, he came back resolved to give his whole life to mission work among the down-and-outs of Kansas City. He gave up "The Rev. David B. Bulkley" and became plain "Dave, the mission worker." He opened a small mission on North main street, and, as he preached and prayed and worked, he saw the need of a place, some sort of a house, with beds, where he could take men whose lives had been changed—drunkards, thieves, men just out of the penitentiaries, men who, through the work of the mission, had caught a new vision but had nowhere to stay.

One of the directors of the mission was Frank Ennis, a coffee wholesaler. A few years before, he had bought for $5,000 the old bawdy house of Madam Lovejoy at the northwest corner of Third and Wyandotte streets, a stone mansion of three stories and twenty-four rooms, built in the '80s. It had been vacant for years, ever since the moral revolution had wiped out the segregated district of this city.

For fifty years that house, with its round spire pointing upwards, had been a landmark of vice in this city. It and the house of Annie Chambers, adjoining it on the north, and the house of Eva Prince next to it on the west, had been the three most notorious houses of that kind in the "red-light district." Salvation Army workers thereabouts used to call them "gilded palaces of sin." And the three women who owned and conducted those three houses were known as "the queens of the red-light."

Mr. Ennis had bought the house as a real estate investment. It is said it cost Madam Lovejoy $100,000 to build. So, to Ennis went Dave Bulkley and proposed that the house be leased to the mission.

"You know," he said to Ennis, "there are at least four penitentiaries pouring into this city men who have just finished their prison terms. Those men are bewildered after having been so long in prison. They should have a quiet place in which to live for awhile until they find themselves, where I can work with them, pray with them, point them to a better life. I want a quiet place to which I can take a drunkard who is trying to reform, and stand with him until he is able to walk alone. You know, Mr. Ennis, a man who has been a criminal or who has been downed by drink or bad habits, and has caught a new vision in our mission, who sees God in the mists, is like a child just learning to walk. I want a place where I can keep him and nurse him along."

So, Ennis leased to him the old Lovejoy house at a small rental. Dave had a good home in a respectable neighborhood and he gave that up and went with his wife and little girl to live in the old gilded palace.

"But, you mustn't take your wife and little girl to live among those people," protested his friends. "To get the best results I must live with those men," said Dave Bulkley.

And in the room of Madam Lovejoy, on the first floor, with the trap door in the corner through which she used to draw up the wine and other liquors from the iced troughs in the cellar, Dave and his wife and daughter set up housekeeping. And in the other rooms were drunkards trying to reform, men out of prison only a few days, men staggering to their feet from all sorts of knock-out blows, men who had lost heart in the battle of life—all sorts of beaten men. . . .

Next door to the west was the old Eva Prince house, yet filled with women of the underworld, the very scum of it. One day one of those women came to the Lovejoy house and knocked timidly on its front door. Mrs. Bulkley saw her standing there and opened the door. The woman was weeping. Her baby was dead, her baby of the underworld, fatherless, because she did not know who its father was, but she had lavished all the love of her heart, starved for love, upon that baby, and after it died she had kept it in her room until the other women convinced her that it must be buried. Then she came to Mrs. Bulkley.

"My baby was never bad," she said. "I am down and out. No woman was ever worse than I am, but my little baby was pure and I want her buried like any other good baby, with a funeral sermon. Do you think Mr. Bulkley would preach a funeral sermon over my baby?" "Yes, he would be glad to," answered Mrs. Bulkley. And so, one day the baby was brought into the gilded old dance hall of the Lovejoy mansion.

I remember that dance hall. In the days, many years ago, when I was a police reporter, early one morning came word that a man had committed suicide in the Lovejoy place. With the policemen I rode up there and went in. From the ceiling of the dance hall, hung a costly chandelier of gilded metal and cut glass that sparkled in the electric light, and from it hung the body of a man. After a night of drink and debauchery he had arisen quietly and crept stealthily down, drawn a chair under the chandelier, tied his suspenders to the chandelier and around his neck and kicked the chair away. And there he hung, his body twirling slowly this way and that, reflected a hundred times in the mirrors of French plate that lined the walls, in the very spot where he had danced the night before.

I have forgotten his name, but I shall never forget the looks of horror on the chalky faces of those girls who stood in that garish place staring at that figure.

And there, beneath that chandelier the coffin of the Magdalen's baby was placed and the mother and many men and women of the underworld gathered for the funeral. . . .

Dave preached the funeral of the baby that day and the scores of women who had come in, many of whom had never heard a sermon for years, wept and sobbed.

There was one listener to that sermon that no one knew was listening. The rear of the old mansion of Annie Chambers backs up close to the rear of the Lovejoy place. Annie, now ninety-two years old, her hands knotted with rheumatism, almost blind, alone in her big house, the windows in her gaudy dance hall darkened, sitting there with her memories, had heard of the funeral that was to be held in the Lovejoy house next door. And when the hour came she climbed the stairs of her house, and so reached a back window. Gently she raised the sash, so no one would hear, and there she stood listening. It was the first sermon she had heard since she was a girl, more than seventy-five years ago.

"But it wasn't the first time I had wept in seventy-five years," Annie Chambers said to me yesterday. "People think women of my sort are hard-hearted, but we have hearts, too, and sometimes they melt in sorrow. But we hide it from the world, for our business requires us to put on a gay front. I know what it is to sob myself to sleep, many a time. And so I wept when I heard Mr. Bulkley preach. I knew he must be a good man, and my soul was stirred as never before. When they carried the baby out, I could hear that poor mother weeping and I knew her own sorrow because, when I was a good woman and wife, away back there in the beginning of things, I had two babies of my own that died."

So, after the funeral, Annie Chambers crept down the stairway to her own memories of seventy years as a "madam" of the red-light. . . . The strange funeral of the babe in the harlot's house rang in her ears. She began to watch the doings of Bulkley and his wife. . . .

One evening last summer a whisky still blew up in the neighborhood . . . and among those who went out to watch were Mrs. Bulkley and Annie Chambers. They met there on the sidewalk and began to talk, and Mrs. Chambers said: "I know what you have been doing. I have been watching you. I heard the sermon your husband preached over that woman's baby. . . ."

So began a close friendship between Mrs. Chambers and the

Bulkleys. The Bulkleys were her next door neighbors and they visited her often. Mrs. Bulkley, a good cook, would take dainties over to the aged woman. They gave her a Bible. They prayed with her regularly. One day Mrs. Chambers went to an old trunk and took from it a string of beads of solid gold and gave them to Mrs. Bulkley for her little daughter. Another time early this winter Mr. and Mrs. Bulkley were going to a conference at the Moody Bible Institute in Chicago and Mrs. Chambers said: "My dear, you will freeze up there with that thin coat you have on." So she went to an old chest and took out a coat of real Alaskan seal that had laid there in moth balls for years . . . and draped it over the shoulders of Mrs. Bulkley. . . .

Three weeks ago Annie Chambers sent for Mr. Bulkley and his wife and said she wished to deed her property to them for the mission. She owned it outright. . . . She thought it would be a good place for a refuge or home for girls who needed love and sympathy.

"You don't know what it means to me in my last days to have someone to love and care for me," said Annie Chambers. "You have made me supremely happy. I have been thinking lately that there are many women who need just such love and sympathy to save them. And I want to give you this big house of mine for that purpose. It has twenty-four rooms and all I want is that it shall be used for that purpose, and that I be allowed to live in my own room here. . . ."

"We want to make you happy to the very last," said Mrs Bulkley. "You have made me the happiest woman in Kansas City," she answered. "Each night I kneel down by my bed and pray. I tell God what He already knows, that I have been a disobedient woman, that my life has been all wrong nearly all my long life, and I ask Him if it is possible that He can forgive a woman like me."

"He loves to forgive," said Mrs. Bulkley. "Haven't I read to you the story of how He forgave the woman who had done wrong and said to her 'go thou and sin no more.'"

"Yes, and I know He has forgiven me, for it says in that good book that He forgives and forgets all the bad past. I feel that He has forgiven me and with that thought I fall asleep and sleep as soundly as a little child. I am looking to the future, not to the past. I can't undo the wrongs I have done, but I have some little time left in which to make what amends I can, and in giving this property to the mission I am making amends. I wish I had more to give."

Conclusion

Today, the City Union Mission is large, with many effective programs. Mrs. Bulkley started a women's program and a children's program, including camp.

Many rescue ministries have started in former brothels—the red velvet, gold-trimmed furniture somehow seems romantic. But there is nothing romantic about selling or buying sex. Today the pimp stands in the shadows of the streets watching his "property"—young girls or boys—selling. They jump in a car—off they go—and are back on the street in a little while. One could get discouraged and say there is no hope. But that is not what Mrs. Bulkley did, once she denied self, gave up her comfortable lifestyle, and started to follow Jesus to the most hurting people. Satan was on the run. The same light that shone in their home in the mission—those old halls of prostitution—still shines on the streets today where the power of God's love draws the Christian worker to the sinner waiting to be rescued.

There are today some parts of cities where the devastation is so bad I can't believe it is America, and yet that same light, the light of the world—Jesus—calls people to do crazy things.

"God is calling me to start a mission in New Orleans. . . ." "You're crazy," his young wife said. But it wasn't long ago that my husband and I went to visit the new expansion project of the IUGM. The building had been abandoned and it was in a violent, desolate area. There was no running water and one bare light bulb. As the missionary took us through the building with a flashlight, he said, "Here we are going to have our dining room, this is where the stainless steel kitchen will be, the library, the dorm, the chapel. . . ." We came back to where his wife was. Their two children were playing on a blanket. She said, "I have to keep them on the blanket, it's so dirty in here and they could get hurt." Today their vision is a reality, with a budget over $400,000. People are fed, the Gospel is heard, and lives are changed.

$\mathscr{B}e$ $\mathscr{S}$trong and $\mathscr{C}$ourageous

Mabel Eberhardt
Photo used with permission of the Washington Post

*Be strong and courageous. . . . God goes with you; he will never leave
you nor forsake you.* —Deuteronomy 31:6

*Be strong and of good courage; be not afraid, . . . for the LORD thy God is
with thee whithersoever thou goest.* —Joshua 1:9 KJV

*Teach the older women to be reverent in the way they live. . . . Then they
can train the younger women to love their husbands and children, to be
self-controlled and pure, to be busy at home, to be kind, and to be
subject to their husbands.* —Titus 2:3–5

Introduction

 $\mathcal{T}$ he race riots of the 1960s had already killed four people in our
town. The mission where Steve and I lived with our five-year-
old son stood in the middle. The white neighborhood was on one
side, the black neighborhood on the other. There were bullet holes
in the side of the mission. Where would Jesus be? Right there, where
His love could heal the hate! God had led us to start a daily youth
program, and our bus picked up kids out of those violent, hot neighborhoods. We had hired a college student who, along with teaching
swimming and crafts, told the kids about the love of God.

My husband had been accused of starting a riot. Two men came
to the mission carrying guns. One wanted to kill him; the other
wanted to arrest him. By the time we got to the annual International Union of Gospel Missions convention, I was discouraged,
tired, and weary. Mabel Eberhardt, who was old, wise, and loving,
befriended me and took me under her motherly wing. I poured out
my heart to her and asked her to pray for our family. She listened a
lot, talked a little, and agreed to pray. That felt good, and I knew I
could trust her. After the convention and for years, she mailed us
notes of encouragement. They would come at just the right time.
Years later, I found Titus 2:3 and 4: "Older women . . . train the
younger women."

≈Ω⊙℘≈

Mabel Julia Kramer was born August 19, 1892. As her mother
tenderly cared for her, she often prayed for her. Little did her mother
know that in the next century Mabel would impact thousands of lives
for Christ, including ours and our children. Mabel's mothering heart
developed through knowing the Scripture and applying it to life ex-
periences. In Mabel's words:

> In August 1906 my mother was a delegate to the Women's
> Missionary Society . . . and she took me with her. While
> listening to a sermon on Romans 12:1, "I beseech you
> therefore, brethren, by the mercies of God, that ye present
> your bodies a living sacrifice, holy, acceptable unto God,
> which is your reasonable service." I knew that was what I
> wanted to do. I surrendered my life to the Lord when Dr. G.
> B. Kimmel had the closing invitation. . . . I joined the church
> that fall, and attended the revival where Herbert Eberhardt
> was converted (page 2).[1]

Herbert and Mabel dated during high school and college. They were married and then attended seminary together. He became pastor of a church, and they had two children (p. 4).

The Eberhardts were called to the work of rescue in 1921. The social conditions during that period were critical. Material help and the love of God were desperately needed during the Roaring 20s with its immorality and the Great Depression, and two World Wars. Mabel's accomplishments were many. God worked in her heart and gave her the strength and courage she needed. In her words:

> The Lord had a special lesson for me. Right at the beginning when my mother was caring for our two children I was working hard preparing Christmas baskets of food for the needy. I had a miscarriage coming down a long flight of steps with a heavy basket. In the hospital I realized how my own family needed me just a few days before Christmas! The Lord surely had to teach me that there are some "priorities" over other "priorities"! Several years later the Lord gave us another son (page 10).

Mabel's first priority became her family, then the mission. When their children were raised, the Lord called the Eberhardts to leave Indianapolis, family, friends, and home to go to the Central Union Mission in Washington, D.C. Fear gripped Mabel's heart when the board wanted her to direct the children's home and the mission camp for inner-city children. Then God worked in her heart during a Sunday school class (page 14). The lesson was on Joshua 1:9.

> Have not I commanded thee? Be strong and of a good courage; be not afraid, neither be thou dismayed: for the LORD thy God is with thee whithersoever thou goest (KJV).

Conclusion

Over the years Mabel Eberhardt's credentials developed as a trainer of young women. She lived a reverent life; she knew and lived the Word. All her children became Christians. She and her husband, married for forty-seven years, were partners in rescue work for forty-one years until Herbert's death. She became an expert on how to mix family and ministry and not lose her own children. This mother of so many was named Mother of the Year. Every mother needs courage to raise children in this world. A godly, wise, and loving woman who knows the joy of God has hope and courage developed over the years. The Scripture proclaims:

We rejoice in the hope of the glory of God. Not only so, but we rejoice in our sufferings, because we know that suffering produces perseverance; perseverance, character; and character, hope (Romans 5:2–4).

May our Lord Jesus Christ himself and God our Father, who loved us and by his grace gave us eternal encouragement and good hope, encourage your hearts and strengthen you in every good deed and word (2 Thessalonians 2:16–17).

Endnotes

The following material may be found at the International Union of Gospel Missions, William Wooley Library, Kansas City, Missouri.

1. Mabel Eberhardt, *The Lord Hath Done Great Things for Us Whereof We Are Glad . . . Psalm 126:3*, a pamphlet.

15

Father to the Fatherless

Doris Nye & Marie Sandvik

Many children are fatherless. Their fathers have died of illness, were killed, are in prison or have abandoned them. They will go to sleep tonight, with tears streaming down their cheeks, wondering, "Why? Why me?" But wait, praise God! The Scriptures are true. He becomes "a father to the fatherless" (Psalm 68:5). God with His great love rescued many fatherless children who learned to put their hurts in the hands of God.

Introduction

*M*arie Sandvik was born in Sogn, Norway and was raised by her grandmother. People thought she was odd and called her "the crazy kid." Unless otherwise noted, the information in this chapter is taken from *To the Slums with Love* by Marie Sandvik and Doris Nye (Minneapolis: Marie Sandvik Center, 1970).

The Haugeans, a pietist group in the Lutheran Church, were strong in Sogn. Their preaching of salvation now appealed to little Marie's desire for reality. She walked up to the well-known Ludvig Hope, then a young man, and told him she was giving her heart to the Lord. The young Hope smiled, put his hand on her head and dedicated her to the work of the Gospel. "This little girl is going to move mountains," he said. She stood there in wooden shoes, ankle length dress, and long blond Norwegian hair. She felt like she could move "Helvetesberget," (Hell's mountain) near her home.

From that moment on, Marie knew her heavenly Father loved her. If she was the only little girl on earth, He would have sent His son, Jesus, to die for her. Perfect love had come into her hurting life. She put her little hand of faith into her heavenly Father's hand, and He led her to America when she was seventeen. She was one of thousands of immigrants that flooded America in the early 1900s.

The teenage newcomer girl sobbed her heart out. The pillow was drenched in bitter, salty tears. "I am so hungry. My stomach hurts. The only food I have had today is a White Castle hamburger and a cup of coffee. My ragged gingham dress can't last much longer, and my shoes are all worn out. Kjare Gud! And I thought money grew on trees in America."

Marie's school teacher taught her English, and Marie worked her way through high school, college, and seminary. She washed pots and pans in a restaurant and edited the Norwegian magazine *Nordvestern*. She also sold magazines on the streets of Minneapolis in the slums. In Marie's words:

I was selling magazines, . . . I came to a mission, and looked in and saw its darkness. The people inside looked lonely. And I was lonely too. I told myself that when I finished college I was going to start a place so the poor people can come in.

After seminary Marie became a church parish worker and traveled doing evangelistic work. It wasn't until her late thirties she heard the story of a hurting little girl in the slums of Minneapolis. She remembered her own life of poverty and how God had rescued her. The Holy Spirit made it clear to Marie that she was called to go back "To the Slums with Love" and start a mission. She often quoted C. T. Studd, "Some may prefer to live within the sound of church and chapel bell, but I want to run a rescue shop within a yard of hell." In 1940 Marie took all the money she had, forty-five dollars, and rented a tavern. She moved in with the rats and cockroaches, and because of her childhood she knew how to live above the circumstances. In Marie's words:

> Poor in American currency I had access to great riches. I was an heir to an estate called the Kingdom of God. I sat in the midst of the grubby ex-tavern fingering through my bank account, Philippians 4:19. "My God shall supply every need of yours." [I went to the] music store, and began telling the piano salesman that God had called me to open a church in the slums. The salesman eyed me warily, but the manager overheard and came towards me smiling. "A church in the slums, eh? And you have a real Norwegian accent. Most of the people in the Gateway are Scandinavians . . ." Then with tears in his eyes, he told about the first hymn he had been taught as a child in Norway. "I'll get a piano to you. You can pay for it when you can."

From 1940 to 1990 God supplied Marie's needs as she ministered to women, men, girls, and boys. In 1944 God called a Wheaton College graduate, Doris Nye, to work at her side. Nothing, including changing ethnic population, the riots of the 1960s, or redevelopment could stop these two single women, city missionaries. Ninety homeless men were displaced when the Minneapolis Revival Mission was demolished to make way for new buildings. The mission moved and became the Marie Sandvik Center, and they were able to expand their children's and mothers' work.

> Marie lived dangerously. Once a gun was pointed at her by a drunk soldier who had gone berserk. . . . He was going to shoot himself, he said. . . . "Drop that gun," said Marie. Then he pointed the gun at her. "Get out of here or I will kill you," he screamed. "In Jesus' name drop that gun," Marie thundered. He did. Marie has been chased by drug addicts with switchblades. One day while visiting for vacation Bible

school, she had a pot of urine poured on her head from the third floor of a tenement.

Little Debbie had never heard about Jesus. She came to the mission hungry, hurting, and alone. Her father was in jail; her mother, drunk. When Debbie heard that Jesus loved her she cried big tears. "Dear Jesus, come into my heart," she sobbed. I put my arm around her and assured her that Jesus had come in. Two days later little eleven-year-old Debbie was raped and killed by her mother's drunk boyfriend. . . . If Christ came to Minneapolis . . . He would be coming down the Street of the Poor. He would gather the inner city urchins in His arms saying "Let the children come unto Me." He would bring food to the hungry. Warmth to the shivering. Cheer to the cheerless. Hospitality to the lonely. Assurance to the fearful. Comfort to the mentally disturbed. And to us and to those who have helped, He would say, "Inasmuch as ye have done it unto one of the least of these my brethren, ye have done it unto me" [Matt. 25:40].

Conclusion

Doris Nye reports that today the Marie Sandvik Center has grown to over twenty staff and hundreds of volunteers who work with over five hundred children, one hundred mothers, one hundred street people, and a women's shelter. Marie is with little Debbie and their heavenly Father. God has wiped away all tears from their eyes.

Bibliography

Dolan, Phyllis, "War Comes to the Gateway," *Minneapolis Sunday Tribune*, September 20, 1942.
Luther, Sally, "Hymns and Hot Coffee," *Minneapolis Sunday Tribune*, May 7, 1950.
"The Doris Nye Story," *Minneapolis Tribune*, May 1964.
"An 'Island' of Refuge," *Daily American*, 1968.
"Aftenposten," *Power Magazine*, Oslo, Norway.

16

For Such a Time As This

Susan E. Benjamin

Perfect submission all is at rest,
I in my Savior am happy and blest,
Watching and waiting, looking above,
Filled with His goodness, lost in His love.
                              —Fanny Crosby

Introduction

*W*ould apartheid close the Cape Town City Mission? South Africa's apartheid laws forced separation of the races into separate townships for black, colored, indian, and white. Homes and buildings, including the mission, were bulldozed down. Forced to leave district 6 and find a new home was Susan E. Benjamin, who had been converted years earlier at the mission. "Mommy," as she was known, asked the city missionaries to hold meetings in her home. That was the beginning of a new concept of ministry that swept through the townships. God used this simple woman to perform a critical task at a critical time, which helped keep the mission alive, "for such a time as this" (Esther 4:14). Today the ninety-four-year old mission is one of the largest works among Capetown's poor, with thirteen locations serving thousands.

❧❧❧❧❧

Susan and her husband were heavy drinkers when Jesus rescued them. One only has to look at Susan's worn Bible to know how she got victory in her life. She wrote in it, "Steps to Victory—Romans 3:23, 1 John 1:9, Romans 5:8, John 1:12. Rejoice that He is in you to give you victory day by day." Two of her favorite songs were, "Look and Live—I've a Message from the Lord, Halelujah" and "Blessed Assurance."

Just weeks before the first city mission building was built in a township, during a Mother's Club meeting in her home, "Mommy" went to be with the Lord.

> Blessed assurance, Jesus is mine!
> O what a foretaste of glory divine!
> Heir of salvation, purchase of God
> Born of His Spirit, washed in His blood.
>
> This is my story, this is my song,
> Praising my Savior all the day long;
> This is my story, this is my song,
> Praising my Savior all the day long.
>
> —Fanny Crosby

17

From Generation to Generation

Estelle & Cliff Phillips

Grandma was not out in the open. You always saw Grandpa; but with the Lord, she was the wind under his wings. I admire my Grandma. Without her Grandpa could not have accomplished what he did.
—Dayna Pagard

*I praised and honoured him that liveth for ever,
whose dominion is an everlasting dominion, and his kingdom
is from generation to generation.*
—Daniel 4:34 KJV

Introduction

*O*ur mission family roots are deep and strong, and today our tree keeps on budding all over the world. During social upheaval and migration of people, God has used couples like the Nasmiths, McAuleys, Clarkes, Trotters, and Phillipses to start missions.

~☙◎❧~

America was on the threshold of a new century when Estelle Fithian was born in 1903. Her father was a quiet man, a farmer and carpenter. Estelle was chosen for the prestigious job of the first telephone operator in the area in which she lived. Cliff Phillips met Estelle when he paid a telephone bill, and they were married in 1921. Work was hard to get and Cliff started drinking heavily, "serving the devil and serving him well."[1]

Often there were parties in the Phillips home where alcohol was served. People got sick and Estelle would have to clean up the mess the next morning. Estelle's first baby, Roland, was born with the "shakes" and she was not able to nurse him. Within two weeks her baby boy was dead, but soon they had a little baby girl that lived.

The young couple packed up their old truck and moved to Chicago. Cliff drove a coal truck, did some carpentry, and they both sold pots and pans door to door.

Estelle had been married eleven years when her Christian mother-in-law came to visit.

> There were a lot of changes to be made when [Cliff's] mother came to visit . . . ashtrays to be put away, beer to be removed from the ice box, and worldly literature to be thrown away.[2]

Mom wanted to go to church, so the couple chose a church they thought she would like, Paul Rader's Chicago Gospel Tabernacle. It was there that Cliff went to the altar, and a man opened the Bible and read Romans 10:9–13 to him.

> If thou shalt confess with thy mouth the Lord Jesus, and shalt believe in thine heart that God hath raised him from the dead, thou shalt be saved. For with the heart man believeth unto righteousness; and with the mouth confession is made unto salvation. For the scripture saith, Whosoever believeth on him shall not be ashamed. For there is no difference between the Jew and the Greek: for the same Lord over all is rich unto all that call upon him. For whosoever shall call upon the name of the Lord shall be saved [KJV].

The man asked Cliff, "Do you believe that?" Cliff said, "Yes." The man then asked Cliff, "Are you saved?" Cliff replied, "No, I don't think so." The man then told him, "Read the Scripture and put your own name in there, If thou, Clifford, shalt confess, . . ." The wise counselor took all the time it needed for Cliff to be saved that day.

Two weeks later Estelle was listening to a Christian Businessmen's Committee radio broadcast on the Moody station. The speaker explained how to be born again. At the end of the program he said, "If the Lord is speaking to your heart, kneel where you are and ask Him into your heart." Estelle knelt next to the bathtub and asked the Lord into her heart. He became her Savior, and now her marriage was complete—Estelle, Cliff, and the Lord.

The Phillips' personal relationship with Christ developed and grew as Jesus became Lord of their lives. They studied the Bible and prayed together. In Christ they became new creations. Their interests changed, their home life changed, and what they did with their time changed. They became members of a church where Cliff became chairman of the board. Their church went to the Sunshine Mission regularly to put on services. The Phillipses also became familiar with the work of the Pacific Garden Mission. For ten years God trained Estelle in rescue work and Christian family living. The pattern of their ministry together developed, and Cliff, like David Nasmith, became a man of flaming zeal for the lost and the suffering.

Cliff became a successful building contractor in Chicago. As with the Nasmiths, however, God had a master plan for the Phillips' lives. Hanging onto each other and hanging onto the Lord, they followed God's call and migrated to Fresno, California, in 1945.

Cliff's pastor took him to lunch and showed him "skid row." He said, "Cliff, Fresno needs a rescue mission and you are the man to get it started." Cliff organized a Fishers of Men Club to "do it." Many fine Christian men came and they started to pray for a mission. In 1949 the Fresno Rescue Mission was established and started to grow.

Money was scarce so Cliff agreed to be a "volunteer" director, without a guaranteed income. Living by faith was all very well but . . . one day there was no food in the house. Cliff and Estelle were driving home from the Mission, Estelle was distressed and in tears. Cliff tried to reassure her that everything would be all right. When they arrived home, on the doorstep was a large box of food. . . .

Estelle was the "bookkeeper" of the family and she knew how bad finances were. At times when they were riding in the car she would go on and on about their lack of funds. Cliff would stop the car and say "Let's get on our knees." They would kneel by the car and he would pray, "Please Lord give Estelle more faith to trust in you."

The Mission needed to move to a larger place and would have to increase the budget to $800 for rent. Discussion followed. A board member stated, "It can't be done; we don't have enough money!" Cliff insisted that the ministry had to expand. Another board member, a Christian of only two years, listened for awhile, then offered, "You are both right. We are doing all we can do, but I've been reading in my New Testament in Philippians 4:19 that God will supply all our needs. Now, are we going to do what we can do, or are we going to believe what God can do?" The board voted to increase the rent.

The next day, Cliff Phillips phoned a few men and asked them to attend a prayer meeting. Where? Cliff didn't know. They drove up into the hills, found a large rock under a shady oak tree, and had their prayer meeting. For three hours they sought the Lord's wisdom and blessing in launching out into starting rescue missions in other needy cities.

Cliff and the men at the mission often gave their testimonies of how God saved them and transformed their lives. Cliff often said, "I'm just a sinner saved by grace." These testimonies touched Estelle's heart and tears often came to her eyes as she praised God for His amazing grace.

> Amazing grace—how sweet the sound
> That saved a wretch like me!
> I once was lost but now am found,
> Was blind but now I see.
>
> Thru many dangers, toils and snares
> I have already come;
> 'Tis grace hath brought me safe thus far,
> And grace will led me home.
>
> When we've been there ten thousand years,
> Bright shining as the sun,
> We've no less days to sing God's praise
> Than when we'd first begun.
>
> —John Newton

The twenty-two missions that have their roots in the Phillips' story were built on a strong foundation: the Word of God, transformed lives, and the example of Estelle and Cliff.

The children, women, and family work at the Fresno Rescue Mission was directed by Estelle. The pain she had gone through in the early years of her marriage caused her heart to beat with compassion. Estelle was not judgmental and always had time to listen and pray. She knew that when a husband drank up his pay check, a box of food was only temporary help. Often she prayed with women that God would transform their husbands and remove their thirst for drink.

Practical help and spiritual help went hand-in-hand, as Estelle ministered to the least, the last, the lost. A box of food included a tract with Bible verses. Thursday was clothing day, and mothers were often more concerned about finding clothes for their children than for themselves. But the women looked forward to Estelle's soft-spoken, yet powerful devotions—Bible study. Other Christian women came to help and one of them was Pauline (Pretzer) Baker.

Pauline Pretzer was born in Russia and her family immigrated to California during the Bolshevik Revolution. Years later Pauline's husband drowned. While listening to the mission's radio broadcast, she decided to bring her late husband's clothes to the mission. In Pauline's words:

> As the days and weeks went by, the burden grew greater for those lost and destitute women. . . . I spent as much time as I could at the mission. On Thursdays I help with the family work; there for the first time in my Christian life I did personal witnessing; a new experience for me, and one that is vitally necessary for mission work. Proverbs 11:30, "The fruit of the righteous is a tree of life; and he that winneth souls is wise."[3]

From generation to generation, Estelle and Cliff had volunteered in the Chicago missions and learned rescue. Pauline volunteered at the Fresno Rescue Mission and learned rescue work from Estelle and Cliff. Pauline then founded the Evangel Home for homeless women and children and became an advocate for women's ministries on the West Coast and in the IUGM.

Estelle was in the background, quiet, and yet every day was in the battle as she became a great prayer warrior. Prayer was her greatest contribution to rescue work, her husband, family, and all who came in contact with her. She knew well the battle between good and evil within the human heart. She knew God could overcome evil, whether it was one of the men at the mission tempted to get a drink, or Pauline trembling with fear over the task God called her to.

The similarities between the Phillipses and Nasmiths are striking. David Nasmith and Cliff Phillips often proclaimed, "But for the grace of God there go I," and they both shared their Savior with everyone they met. Frances Nasmith and Estelle Phillips were both 100 percent behind their husbands and equal to them in their love for the Lord, others, and missions. Their homes were the center of their ministries and places where laughter, fellowship, good food, and love could be found. When David and Cliff came home, it was to places of refreshment and peace. Both women were alone a lot and had time to think and pray while their husbands were out in the whirlwind of starting new missions in growing cities.

Estelle wrote poetry sometimes as she waited for Cliff. One day while waiting at the mission, she wrote,

> As I sit here in the office,
>   looking out upon the street,
> Seeing buildings round about us . . .
>   tumbling down into defeat.
> These old walls hold precious memories,
>   so much has happened in this place.
> Lives of men, women and children,
>   have been transformed by God's dear grace.
> It has been our precious privilege,
>   His dear word to them we've told,
> Telling them that Jesus loves them,
>   and they, too, could enter the fold.
> Oh, there is Leo filled with wine and dope,
>   all the way from Mexico.
> Gave his heart to the Lord one night,
>   then back to his people he did go.
> *Arnold Thiesen! Ah! Oh, so hopeless,
>   business, family, friends all gone.
> Led to Jesus by a doctor,
>   was faithful here and many won.
> †Lester Myers, a big gambler,
>   broke and needing a place to stay.
> Arnold led him to the Savior in a prayer group,
>   such as we had today.

---

* Arnold Thiesen started the San Diego (CA) Rescue Mission.
†Les Myers married Pauline, and they started the San Jose (CA) Rescue Mission (now City Team).

‡John Drizewicki, a Catholic lad,
weary, tired and without hope.
Met the Savior one day in the basement,
as he was chipping up some soap.

At the end of Estelle's life, her frail body lay in bed, physically unable to perform simple tasks; her mind and speech were gone. She forgot everything and everyone around her. However she never forgot the Lord! If someone started a Bible verse or a Christian song, she would finish it. As her physical systems were shutting down, her spirit was getting stronger. Her daughter was holding Estelle in her arms, singing Christian songs, when she died in 1988. Cliff died shortly thereafter.

Outwardly we are wasting away, yet inwardly we are being renewed day by day. So we fix our eyes not on what is seen, but on what is unseen. For what is seen is temporary, but what is unseen is eternal (2 Corinthians 4:16, 18).

We . . . prefer to be away from the body and at home with the Lord (2 Corinthians 5:8).

Well done, good and faithful servant! (Matthew 25:23).

We are surrounded by such a great cloud of witnesses (Hebrews 12:1).

Conclusion

Like Estelle Phillips we can be committed with courage, "compassion, kindness, humility, gentleness and patience. . . . And over all these virtues put on love . . ." (Col. 3:12–14). Then we can look forward with joy to the next century knowing that, from generation to generation, in cities around the world, women and men have obeyed God's commands of love.

Thou shalt love the Lord thy God with all thy heart, and with all thy soul, and with all thy mind. This is the first and great commandment and the second is like unto it, Thou shalt love thy neighbor as thyself. On these two commandments hang all the law and the prophets (Matthew 22:37–40 KJV).

---

‡John Drizewicki is the Executive Director of the Boise (ID) Rescue Mission.

I will put my laws in their minds and write them on their hearts. I will be their God, and they will be my people (Hebrews 8:10).

For God so loved the world that he gave his one and only Son, that whoever believes in him shall not perish but have eternal life (John 3:16).

The impact of Estelle and Cliff Phillips is still felt throughout the West Coast, for today there are missions in San Jose, San Diego, Stockton, Bakersfield, Sacramento, Marysville, Indio, Watsonville, Redding, Santa Rosa (all in California); Klamath Falls and Medford (Oregon); Ogden, Utah; Yuma and Phoenix (Arizona) that all relate to the Phillipses and their converts, and this list is not all inclusive. City Team (formerly the San Jose Rescue Mission) is now one of the largest missions in America. God had just the couple, simple folks, who went west like many Americans and took the message of salvation and love for the poor and broken with them—and planted seeds for the kingdom.

⚜

> To God be the glory, great things He hath done,
> So loved He the world that He gave us His Son,
> Who yielded His life an atonement for sin,
> And opened the life-gate that all may go in.
> O perfect redemption, the purchase of blood,
> To every believer the promise of God;
> The vilest offender who truly believes,
> That moment from Jesus a pardon receives.
> Praise the Lord, praise the Lord,
> Let the earth hear His voice!
> Praise the Lord, praise the Lord,
> Let the people rejoice!
> O come to the Father, thro' Jesus the Son,
> And give Him the glory—
> Great things He hath done.
> —Fanny J. Crosby

Endnotes

1. Richard W. Anderson, *All Things to All Men* (Winona Lake, Ind.: The Rodeheaver Hall-Mack Company, 1966), 55.
2. Ibid., 52.
3. Pauline Myers, *How to Establish a Mission or Home for Women* (West Coast Training School of the IUGM, 1965).

If you would like to start a mission
and help change the heart of your city, please write:

IUGM
1045 Swift Street
Kansas City, MO 64116-4127

Index

➤ ◄